Compliments of God

My love and gratitude to my high-school classmate

Pam Turpin Crocker

for sharing her idea and for the confidence she has

always had in my ability to make it happen

Compliments of God

Copyright © 2014 Julo Spencer

ISBN 978-1-939351-99-9

Acknowledgements

A big hug and thank you to my publisher, Nancy Pendleton at Woodwind Press, for sharing the excitement of writing and making my book come to life.

My ever so grateful love to my editors, Diane Miller and Susan Box, who spent hours helping me. Thank you from my heart.

Thanks to my social media friends for their positive and heartfelt comments that encourage me daily to continue to write, sometimes even requesting something special for a friend or family member. I hope I lived up to their standards as a child of God and used all the right words to comfort them.

My love to my sweetest and best friends, Glenda, Shirley, Diane, Janice and Debbie. They are my sisters in Christ. Thank you for our one-on-one ministries to each other, for keeping me on track and for sharing your love of God with me.

To my brothers, Tommy, Bill and Michael who taught me how to truly love from the heart regardless of how many years, situations, or distance separated us.

A special love and thank you to Gunnar, my step-son. The years of nurturing and experiencing motherhood have sometimes been challenging, but the sight of the young man I see today, has brought me more joy and pride than any discourse between us over the years.

And lastly, my deepest love and gratitude to the man who stole my heart, Duncan, my unbelievably supportive and loving husband. He truly is a gift from above, and only God could love him more. I cannot imagine my life without him.

Introduction

I have always loved the Lord and I have prayed to Him since I was a little girl. When I was about nine years old, I was saved when attending church with a friend of mine on a Wednesday night. Afterward, I invited the pastors to visit the house to talk with my mom and dad about what I had done. I was proud. But when the pastors arrived a few days later, my mother told them I did not know what I was doing at the time and that I didn't even know what it meant to be saved. She quickly dismissed them. Needless to say I was very much embarrassed by my mother's actions so I learned to pray in silence in fear of upsetting her or being scolded. In fact, sadly, I never let anyone hear me pray nor did I ever speak of the Lord our God.

It wasn't until I was in my twenties that I even had a Bible of my own. It was given to me by a man that gets a lot of credit from me for changing my life. He encouraged me to read it and with each page I read, I realized how many answers to life are written in that Book. Forty years later, I still have it; kept by my bedside.

My book is full of prayers and stories that will take you from the darkness to the Light. Included are just a few pictures of places and people that have been a part of my life. A life full of ups and downs, backsliding and sometimes doubt. Overall though, I have no complaints and only one regret. I ask that you please take to heart what each page says and share it with someone. You never know when a similar story or a prayer, written with words meant to comfort, will make a difference in that person's day or perhaps their lifetime. The pictures are black and white but use your imagination and paint them in your mind with whatever colors you want. There are no chapters or table of contents; only pages for you to enjoy. Earmark your favorites and return to them when you feel the need to read His words again.

     I have come a long way from being that little girl who prayed silently, to the woman I am today who screams at the top of her lungs GOD IS GOOD! A late bloomer indeed when it comes to my walk with God, my one regret. But the good news is that I have and will continue to walk with Him. He has picked me up, brushed me off and said to me "go, try it again" more times than I can even count. It is His grace and His love that has led me to where I am today. The words I share with others are "compliments of God". Without Him there would be no prayers written or stories to be told. All glory to God!

My Story

If I were putting chapters in this book I would label this Chapter One, because it is about my mother and father; and in fact, the first chapter in my life that led me to the Lord.

My story may appear to be a bit self-pitying to some and all too familiar to others. I can assure you my only intent is to share with everyone my experiences and how the twists and turns of life got me to the place I am at today. If you will hang in there to the end, like I did, you will see my journey was worth the wait and well worth 'the long walk'.

I was the second daughter, the second to the youngest and the least favorite of my mother's five children. Mother never let me forget that I was her ugly duckling and that I would never measure up to my siblings. The boys were the apple-of-her-eye, and my sister was the beauty in the family. There were never any baby pictures of me taken and very few pictures of me as a child exist. I remember my mother always telling the story of when she gave birth to me. My dad had walked into the room and before seeing me, my mom said "Maybe she will straighten out and be one of our beautiful children". Unfortunately, in Mom's mind, that never happened. The earliest picture of me as a baby was taken when I was thirteen months old, and it would be several more years before any others were developed.

The years ahead would prove that being Dorothy's daughter was not an easy task. I wish so much that I had fond memories of my time with Mother as a child. I wanted to please her and for her to praise me and love me in return. I honestly do not remember many, if any, occasions when that happened. Had it not been for my siblings, especially the older ones, I don't know that I would have ever felt loved at all. And as their lives progressed and they began to grow and mature, the time with them diminished also.

I was skinny and had stringy hair that was so baby fine, it wouldn't even hold a pony tail. My clothes hung on me like a board, and no matter how pretty the dress might be, I walked with my head down just about everywhere I went. I was shy and withdrawn from the kids at school and I would count the minutes before class was out so I could run home, often taking the shortest route to get there quicker.

My room was the only place I felt safe; it was the one place I could remove myself from the real world and dream the sweetest of dreams. My imagination would carry me to a land of fantasy where I could conjure up the life I wanted to live. I became beautiful behind the door of my bedroom; someone everyone loved and wanted to be. Sometimes a famous artist, or teacher, maybe even an athlete; and at some point, always a movie star. Life was good in my little world. However, once mother discovered my secret life, she told me I was acting stupid and forbid me from closing my door. But that did not stop my imagination from running wild. At night, just after saying my prayer, I would turn back into my character of the day. It was more difficult because I couldn't be as animated as when I was playing in my room. But my creative mind would allow the fantasies to come to life, with my imaginary movements and thoughts that filled my head until I drifted off to sleep.

Though I loved all my siblings, I was closest to my brother just two years older than me. I truly loved him and probably wanted to please him as much as I did my mother. We played army together, crawling around on the ground as if in combat, with our large sticks as our "machine guns". We would sit in the front seat of my dad's old car and pretend we were racecar drivers, speeding around the track while making our own sounds of squealing tires and roaring engines. We played board games together and he taught me the strategy of chess and checkers. He was a wonderful big brother and I loved him very much.

One day my mother met me at the door after school. She was holding one of my dresses and showed me that the hem had been partially ripped out. She escorted me to my room where I found a pair of my brother's old jeans and an old shirt on the bed. "If you are going to act like a boy, you can be a boy" were her words. I slowly removed the dress that I had worn to school and just stood there staring at the boys clothes that were lying on the bed. As I reached for the jeans, my mother grabbed my arm and drug me into the bathroom. I saw the scissors laying on the edge of the sink and immediately started begging her not to cut my hair. She ignored my plea and began whacking my hair off. Mother pulled and yanked as the dull scissors made the task at hand more difficult for her. My sobbing only made matters worse, and she slapped my face and blamed me for the end result of the mess of uneven hair hanging from my head.

My hands had been covering my face to keep the hair from falling into my eyes and mouth. When Mother was done, I leaned over and washed my face with cold water and without looking in the mirror, I turned to walk back to my room. I slowly dressed in the boy's clothes as I had been instructed to do. I tucked the red plaid flannel shirt into the jeans that were at least two sizes too large for me, with the hope of filling them up. I buttoned and zipped and pinned them as tight as I could but still they fell to the floor. No matter, I was still sent outside to play. I went to the side of the house and just sat there so no one could see me and waited until I heard my mother call us in for the evening.

My mother had removed the dresses from my closet, so the clothes I had worn the night before, were to be worn again, only to school now. My brother did all he could to help me. He gave me the only belt he had and helped me cinch the pants to keep them up around my waist. We rolled the pant legs up, and he told me to go to school early so I could get there before the other kids saw me. I did just that. My teacher had arrived to class early, but the door was locked. When I knocked, she came to the door, and without the blink of an eye she let me in. She never asked a single question. She simply moved my desk up behind hers so the class could not see me well and told them that I was her helper for the day. She left the room briefly that morning, and I assume it was to ask one of the other teachers to help her with her class during recess and lunchtime.

As she dismissed the other 26 kids from the room, she looked at me and winked and asked if I would stay and help her some more. She kept me after school long enough for the classroom to clear and the other children to be well on their way home. I gathered my things from my desk, and as I was walking out the door she hugged me and handed me a sealed envelope that had my mother and dad's name on the front of it. I gave it to Mom that night. I don't know exactly what it said, but the dresses were returned to my closet and no mention of the boys clothes were ever made again.

Bubba, my brother, rescued me as often as he could from embarrassing moments caused by my mother. She belittled and made fun of my appearance constantly. She told me I was ugly and called me stupid in front of others as if it were her favorite pastime. Bubba was so caring, and his kind heart would defend me as he would try to make light of her snide remarks.

Mom made me come out of my room one night when we had a house full of company. I was dressed in a thin white gown, ready for bed, and I did not want to go out there in front of anyone since you could see through it. She insisted that I come out and loudly pointed out I had nothing for anyone to see. My brother grabbed a blanket and wrapped it around both of us and asked me to come and watch TV with him. He helped with my homework when he could. We even tried to cook together sometimes which always turned into a disaster; something we laugh about to this day. He once reached over and grabbed a hand full of green peas that were on my plate and ate them for me because he knew I hated them but would not be excused from the table until they were gone. We laugh now about how Mom probably knew what he had done, but the evidence had been eaten so there was no way to find me guilty. He was the only one that really knew I was different from our other siblings. He was my hero and I now know, he was my best friend.

My parents divorced when I was ten. They decided that it was best for me to live with my mother and for my brothers to live with my dad. Their logic was that boys belong with their father and girls with their mother. My older sister and oldest brother had already moved away and married, leaving me the only child in my mother's house. Sadly, my best friend was gone and I was left alone.

My brothers moved in with my dad, my step-mother and her four children. Their lives changed drastically and I was soon just a small memory to them. The visitation with daddy did not take place as the courts had ordered; so as expected, we all grew apart.

Mom worked as a waitress at night in a local bar; so even being an only child, so to speak, our time together as mother and daughter was rare. However, there is one night I recall when she and I were out together. I don't recollect where we had gone, but, I do remember the ride back home quite clearly. It was winter and mother was dressed up for an engagement she had later that evening; the one night a week she was off work. I can still see her in my mind, wearing her Mouton fur and how the street lights made her rhinestone earrings sparkle like diamonds. She was beautiful, and I remember thinking she looked like a movie star that night. As we drove back toward the house we came upon an accident that appeared to have caused some injuries. Mom said to me that she was glad we had not been a minute sooner getting to that spot because that could easily have been us in the accident. She actually cringed at the thought and pulled me close to her, put her arm around me, and hugged me tightly. It was the first time I remember my mother saying she loved me. Though my mother probably forgot that night, I never did.

Because my mom worked nights and I was in school during the day, our paths seldom crossed. I learned quickly to fend for myself. I grew up fast, somewhat unhappy, and very much afraid to be in the house at night alone. The house was dark and only one light at a time was allowed on inside the house. I checked the doors time and time again to make sure they were locked. I stayed up as late as possible, with the TV on, to muffle the sound of the things that go bump in the night; falling asleep on the couch, until the sound of the national anthem playing or the horrendous buzz of the station signing off for the evening would blast and wake me up. It would have upset mother to come home and find me on the couch asleep, so reluctantly I made the trek down the dark hallway to my bedroom. The lamplight in the living room would allow just enough light to get me to where the hallway turned toward my room. I would feel my way along the wall until I felt the built in shelf that the telephone sat on, then turn to my right, take two steps, reach to my left and click the light switch on as quickly as possible. I made sure I had everything ready for the next day of school before turning my light off and jumping quickly into bed. I would close my eyes, clasp my hands together, and pray the same prayer I had the night before. "Please, God, let my mom come home early tonight", always followed by promises of being good. Gently, He would let me fall into a dreamless slumber only to awaken me just long enough to hear the sound of my mother coming in for the night.

As time went on, the nights of Momma coming home at all became further and further apart. She was young, beautiful, single, and living life to its fullest. She had a way with men and used every opportunity she could to get what she wanted, when she wanted it. She would often bring strangers home with her after work. The loud laughter, the vile language, and the inappropriate foolishness would keep me awake, silently crying and praying that they would leave. I could hear sounds coming from my mother's room that I did not understand, but I knew what was going on was not right. I was embarrassed even lying in the darkness alone. When I tried to talk to my mother about how it bothered me, she shunned me and told me "that's too bad. You'll just have to get over it".

I could tell I was nothing more than an inconvenience to her and sometimes I would go days without seeing her, spending night after night alone, going to bed hungry and crying myself to sleep. My whining and crying about needing someone with me only infuriated her, and she would slap my face, as she would say, "to give me something to cry about". Then one day she was gone. Without telling me, I came home from school and mother had moved out of our house. She left a note and said I was to go live with my dad. I took what little I had and walked the ten blocks, to my dad's house and handed him the note.

Daddy had remarried a woman who had four children of her own and my two brothers made six. Now with me, there were seven, and I believe, my being there, only angered my step-mother. The blended family had become accustomed to each other and the ways of life with step-parents and step-siblings. Being different from all the others, I was of course the outcast and alone in a house full of people. I wore hand-me-down clothes that were much too large for me, making my skinny little body look even more shapeless than it already did. There were not many days that I did not feel shameful for my appearance. I shared a bed with a step-sibling who slept hard and wet the bed more often than not. My first night at my dad's house, I was spanked for waking him and my step-mother, to let them know the sheets were wet. This was not a one-time incident and something that had apparently been an issue for quite some time; and, unbeknownst to me, had become very much accepted by the rest of the family. After weeks of trying to sleep on urine-soaked sheets I snuck out of my dad's house and ran back to my mother's. When my dad found me, he beat me, leaving me black and blue from my waist to the back of my legs, down to the knee.

My heart was broken because I was no longer daddy's little girl. Time apart and the influence of my step-mother had made him come to dislike me as much as my mother did. It was as if he had accepted his step-children as his own, and I was now a stranger; a burden that had been handed over to him like an unwanted kitten. I was blamed for things I didn't do or say. There were repeated nights of interrogation by my dad and step-mother. I was deprived of dinner if I did not answer a question to their liking...a question they knew I did not know the answer to.

When the black and blue bruises from one beating were almost gone, I would be beaten again for reasons beyond my comprehension. On the weekends, I was literally deprived of sleep by making me sit at the dining room table all day and into the wee hours of the morning. I was threatened with yet another beating if I moved or fell asleep. I wanted to call my mother and tell her I was sorry for whatever I did to make her send me away; but the phone was off limits to me too. My younger siblings were too young to understand what was going on; and the older ones either were not home or would just turn the other way, probably in fear of what would happen if they interfered. Here I was in a house full of people, yet the loneliness was more than I could have ever imagined when I was at my mother's house.

By chance, my oldest brother saw me walking from school one day and stopped to give me a ride home. Afraid, and wanting so badly for someone to know the truth, I burst into tears the moment I saw him. He was unaware of what was going on so when I showed him the bruises from the beating of the night before, he made sure I never went back to my dad's house again. He took me back to my mother's house and told me if I would stay there, he would do what he could to spend some time with me so I would not be alone and he would certainly make sure I was not beaten again. He kept his promise for as long as he could. I have to assume that he told my dad where I was, because I did not hear from Daddy, and it was years before I saw him again. My brother spoke with my mother, and she agreed that she would move back into the house with me. Though the relationship with her had not changed, I remained in her house for several more years.

By the time I was 13, my mother had remarried. My step-father, my Daddy Tom, was a wonderful man. He was fourteen years my mother's junior and only fourteen years older than me. We became close and he had, in my eyes, become "my dad".

Each pay day he would bring a new dress from the store he worked in as a salesman. A man with impeccable taste, he taught me how to dress like a young lady. He was also an excellent cook and did his best to teach me. I would babysit on the weekends and with what I had learned from Tom, I used the money to help keep my appearance up and buy clothes when the funds allowed.

It didn't take long for my mother to begin to feel insecure. The father/daughter relationship I had developed with Tom was soon hindered by Mom's jealousy along with her temper tantrums and ridiculous accusations. She accused me of trying to seduce my dad and take him away from her. He never laid a hand on me. Even the awkward hug was few and far between. The issues my mother had were too far-reaching for Tom to deal with; and loving her with all of his heart, he gave in to her needs and soon distanced himself from me. Once again I was alone.

Browbeaten and ready to prove to her I was worthy of her love, to Mother's delight, I moved away from home at the age of 17.

My high school education was enough to land me a job at a local insurance agency. Seeing potential in me, the owner encouraged me to get my license and become an agent. This would be my career for the next eighteen years. I had come into my own and accomplished a lifestyle for myself that made me proud. Still, my success was somewhat overshadowed by my mother's opinion of me and the way I lived.

Words of jealousy still spewed from her mouth and the belittling never stopped. The names I was called had changed a bit, but the intent behind them and the sting I felt from them was, however, the same.

Through the years, Mother and I went through troubled times, divorces, and tragedy together. One might think it would have brought us closer; but unfortunately, things really never changed between us.

Our times of closeness were superficial and short lived. For me to shed tears was unnecessary so I learned to condition myself to never cry, regardless of the circumstances. Even with the tragedy of me losing my son, I did not cry in front of my mother. Within a week of his death, I was told to lose the long face and move on with my life. We disagreed on too many things, on so many levels, and we would sometimes go years without speaking to one another. But still I wanted nothing more than to please her and for her to like me.

Just months before mother's death in 1999, we reunited for the last time. Things were still rocky between us and I don't think she ever fully learned to accept me for the person I am. But to the contrary, she was able to allow herself to be happy for me and my relationship I had developed with God. In fact, the last Easter Sunday we spent together, she gave me a small gold cross to wear around my neck. At long last, without using words, I believe the gift was her way of expressing her pride and approval of how I had decided to live my life.

I have reached a maturity level now that allows me to accept and understand why mother felt compelled to dislike me the way she did. After years of abuse and neglect from her, I realize my life with her was nothing more than a mirror of her life with her mother.

I saw my grandmother Julo only once in my lifetime so I never really knew her. She was sitting in a chair under a big shade tree in the front of her house. There was a frown on her face, distrust in her eyes, and I could almost see the wheels turning in her head with thoughts of why I was conspiring against her. All she said to me was "do you belong to Dorothy"? Terrified, I did nothing more than shake my head up and down in answer to her.

The image of my grandmother grows more and more vivid in my mind as I get older. I realize now that what I saw that day, in a nutshell, describes my mother. For years I have asked myself, while my mother probably loved me, why didn't she ever really like me? The answer to my question lies in the face of that woman I saw under the shade tree that day, over fifty years ago. I know now, that the apple did not fall far from the tree.

My mother's fears were passed onto me as a child. She was afraid of water so I was not allowed to go swimming and, consequently, I was afraid of water too. Climbing a tree was not tolerated because she was afraid of heights. I was not allowed to spend the night with a friend because she thought we would do something inappropriate; and I certainly was not allowed to have friends over because she did not trust them in our house.

Death was something that was never discussed even when someone in the family passed on. It was basically just announced, and that was the end of that. I was never encouraged to try anything new to overcome the fears she had bestowed upon me. In my mother's opinion, people who went to church were hypocrites and couldn't be trusted, so that was her excuse for us not attending church. In reality I think it was her lack of knowledge of the Bible and the fear of what others might have thought of her that kept her away. And in all honesty, those feelings are probably the reason for her turning the pastors away just days after I was saved, so many years ago. It was her way of protecting me from what she feared and her way of showing me love.

Out of mother's five children, I was the one chosen to experience what she had. Thoughts of my mother move through my mind often, and I wonder why she did not turn to God in her time of need. And then I think, maybe she did. Was this God's plan to lead me to Him? Was it my mother who actually sacrificed for me, through His plan?

I gained strength and determination through my trials. I was able to overcome and endure the doom and gloom I thought I had been dealt in life. In reality I was on my way to a relationship with our Lord…all because my mother did not like me. Yes, I believe this was God's plan to get me here, in this place today, where I belong.

Like many who have lost their mother, I will never forget the day mine died. However, it is the night before that sticks in my mind the most. For me, it was an answer to a lifelong prayer.

I was driving back from a day at the lake with some friends of mine. I called mom to chat with her during my 45 minute drive home. She was in a great mood, happier than I had heard her sound in a long time and surprisingly, she suggested that I come for lunch the next day. She was going to bake me one of her delicious strawberry cakes that I loved.

We chatted about each other's day and mom spoke reminiscently of some of the past years. We laughed together as we recalled them in a totally different way. Before we said good night to each other, Mom said "I love you. You know I love you, don't you"? I said "yes" and told her I loved her too.

Just as she always said she would, Dorothy Evelyn Julo, my mom, died in her sleep sometime before dawn.

I will forever thank God for that night in my life. Mom was at peace and all the world was right.

My mother spoke of the many places in the world she wanted to go and things she wanted to see. But her fear of the unknown, once again prevented her from ever going beyond our home town. Now when I travel I wear the gold cross she gave me around my neck. It is my way of taking her with me.

Dear Lord,

    We are all human, and we all make mistakes. As parents, the hardest decisions come when trying to do what is best for our children and advising them the best way we know how. As adult children, may we think back and understand that our parents were faced with difficult decisions for us, too. They may not have been the best to us, but they were probably thought to be the best for us. We must remember that knowledge is passed from generation to generation and, with each, a new lesson is learned. Thank You, God, for giving me the understanding I need to accept the decisions that were made for me as a child. I pray that parents today use Your word as a guide to teach their children right from wrong. May they lay no blame on their parents for their upbringing, but grow from the experience and learn to live a life of self-worth. May no parent strike a child or belittle them for their shortcomings. May they never lay guilt on their children to manipulate and control them. But rather lead by example, sharing Your word and extending their love to each of their children as You have to us. As the Father of our Savior, Jesus Christ, I pray in His name, for the peace of all children, young and old. Amen.

Compliments of God

Dorothy Evelyn Julo-Binnion

Julo Spencer

Compliments of God

Prayers To Honor

Dear God,

    Thank You for creating men and women that are willing to risk their life by serving our country. May all that have served, are serving today and all that sacrificed their lives so WE may live FREE, be remembered not just today, but every day. Bless the families of the lost and wounded and let them know we will never forget. Thank You Lord for our freedom. In Jesus' name, amen.

    My special thanks to my dad, my brother Bill, my nephew Randy and my husband Duncan for their time served. Thank you God for bringing all of them home safely.

WWII- Daddy in the center

GOD BLESS THIS NATION

    Do not throw up your hands in despair or disinterest. Renew your devotion to conforming the world to the true and the good. Anything that is lovely is a target for the fallen angels; fall, also, on your knees in prayer for our country and its government. Beg God to shed His grace on America and to mend her every flaw. Take your God-given civic responsibility seriously, as an obligation to protect the rights of men and women, granted by God. When you vote for change in our country, vote with God in mind. He is the country's Leader and we must elect the secondary leaders according to God's word. And when the election is over and a man or woman has been chosen to lead our country, pray that our Lord will provide that person with guidance to restore our nation to the morals it was founded on.

Dear Lord,

Thank you for the kids of the world. Each one, an individual that is precious in Your eyes. I ask that You bless them all with the riches of Your hand. May they have good health, happy and loving families, role models they can look up to; and, of course guidance and Your protection from the evil ways of the world. Please Lord, reach out and touch them and provide their every need. I know they will be safe while on Your watch. Thank You God for the gift of these little angels on earth. In the name of Jesus, Amen

THE DAY AFTER

December 15, 2012

There are so many emotions this time of year. Some make you a bit sad while others make you smile. Today' of course, I am still thinking of yesterday's tragedy and how this time of year will be hard for some to face in the future. Tom, my step-dad, the man that helped raise me and the man I loved as my father, died suddenly on Christmas Eve in 1994. My mother was devastated so I made her my main focus during that time. It took me two weeks to finally slow down to grieve a bit for the loss of my dad. The following year was hard on my mom as she did not want to celebrate the holidays. Two years later I finally talked her into a tree and exchanging gifts in hopes that I could get her back to some normalcy with a little happiness in her life. It's what Tom would want for her because she loved the Christmas season so very much. Mom went to be with the Lord and Tom, the love of her life, in 1999. So it is with mixed emotions I smile and think of mom and Tom this time of year.

I pray that the people that lost a friend or family member yesterday in Connecticut will also be able to have their time to grieve and heal and at some point find a way to enjoy this time of year again and remember their loved one with a smile.

In memory of the victims at

Sandy Hook Elementary

Law and Order

When my husband's son, Gunnar, was six years old, he was fascinated with the authority figures of society. Anytime he saw a police car or fire truck parked somewhere I knew the next words out of his mouth would be "can we go look up close?" If time allowed, we would stop just long enough to take a peek. I can still envision his facial expressions as his eyes would widen with the awe of all that was attached to the vehicle. One day I decided to surprise him with a tour of a REAL police and fire department. I asked a friend that was the chief at one of our local departments if he would help me out. He was more than accommodating to Gunnar with the tour, even taking us behind the scenes where the dispatcher sits and then into the garage where the motorcycles and squad cars are kept. The fire department was located just next to the police department and they were equally able to accommodate Gunnar's curiosities. When it was all said and done, the little wide-eyed boy was handed a round token that resembled a badge. He raised his right hand and swore to be the best deputy around. For years he shared that token with his friends, stating that he was a deputy, a real deputy! That badge is now pasted in his scrapbook along with these memories.

Compliments of God

Dear Lord,

I want to pray for all the police officers, fire fighters, paramedics and those associated with our "public heroes" that are involved in the administration and operation of the rescue teams that help others on a daily basis. Through Your Son, You gave us a marvelous example of charity and the great commandment of love for one another.

John 15:12 "This is my commandment, that you love one another, just as I have loved you".

Please bless these that so generously devote themselves to helping others; sometimes risking their life as they work to protect our families and friends. Grant them courage when they are afraid, wisdom when they must make quick decisions, strength when they are weary and compassion in all they do. You have given them a special talent in this life, and they play a very important role in the ministry by faithfully serving You. I thank You for the gift of these amazing public servants. Through Christ our Lord, I ask that You please watch over them. Amen.

Matthew 5:9 Blessed are the peacemakers, for they shall be called sons of God.

Psalms 138:7 Though I walk in the midst of trouble, you preserve my life; you stretch out your hand against the wrath of my enemies, and your right hand delivers me.

Honoring Veterans Day

Dear Lord,

    I ask that not just today but every day we show our gratefulness to all men and women who have courageously given themselves to keep us safe and free. Our nation has set aside this day to pay tribute to many that have sacrificed for our good. Please God, let each and every one of us honor those that fought, that fight today and that have died for our freedom. May we let their examples inspire our own endeavors by willfully giving ourselves, helping others in a time of need and giving You the glory of creating a better world for all. In Jesus' precious name, we pray. Amen. God bless the U.S.A.

Compliments of God

Kris Etheridge, United States Army
7 years, 9 months

SUMMERTIME AT LAST!
CONGRATULATIONS TO SENIORS!

Dear Heavenly Father,

Thank you for the gained knowledge of our children. I pray that You will show them how to use it wisely. Grant them faith, courage and purpose so they will serve you in effective ways. Father, may all Your children always be aware that knowledge comes from learning, but wisdom comes from You. Now that school is out, may it be a fun and blessed summer for all. Thank You for our graduating seniors. May You always be the One that they follow down the path to their future. In Jesus' name. Amen.

Independence Day

Dear Almighty God,

    As we celebrate Independence Day, may we come to You in thanksgiving for our United States of America. You have bestowed upon our nation the gift of freedom. Laws can divide us, but You unite us because this country was founded on Your Name. We must keep our rights secure by keeping them sacred. IN GOD WE TRUST.

    Many men and women have fought for this country and lost their lives battling for our freedom. Some were old, some were young, but they were all strong and fearless. May we lift up their sacrifice today, our Independence Day, and honor them for not only their courage but for their patriotism. May we be righteous and be granted grace to maintain our liberties and peace. God, let this country always remain in our hearts and give us the strength and knowledge and desire to hold it in safekeeping for our children. I pray as a nation we never fail, that freedom rings and You, our only God, will bless America. In the name of Jesus. Amen.

When I was a young adult, I lived in an apartment. I was preparing something for Thanksgiving Day, the night before the family dinner. I walked into another room, forgetting I had a pan heating on the stove. When I returned, the pan was in flames. I quickly grabbed it to move it from the lit burner. The swift movement of the air created a sudden explosion. Flames sparked the nearby curtains on the kitchen window. In a panic, I called the fire department and ran across to a neighbor's apartment to warn them. The image of the fire I had in my mind was huge and I felt certain the whole complex was going to burn down. I returned to my apartment to see what I could salvage only to find that the curtains were fire retardant and had done nothing other than melt and extinguish themselves. The contents in the pan had completely burned so the fire in the pan had also diminished. All that remained was the smoke and one extremely shameful person. Suddenly, as I stood there feeling relief, my apartment was invaded by firefighters…nine to be exact. Embarrassment rushed over me as I began to apologize to them for my foolishness in making them come out for such a small job caused by nothing more than carelessness. Only kind words were spoken by each of them as they calmed my nerves. I began to feel some pain in my hand and discovered that I had been burned from the small explosion. While the firefighters assessed that things were safe and that we just needed to open windows to air things out, the paramedics began treating my hand to help relieve some of the pain. I was driven to the ER and treated for third-degree burns on my right hand and a portion of my wrist and arm. It took months for my hand to heal; and to this day, although a bit more faded as I get older, the scar still remains. I will never forget how those men responded without question to my cry for help. They earned my total respect for the job they do EVERY DAY for people that are nothing more than strangers. That night in 1981 those nine men were my heroes.

Julo Spencer

West, TX

Dear God,

    As the days after the explosion pass and the memories of that horrid night remain heavy on our hearts, we ask that You keep a watch on the small town of West. We pray for loved ones lost, loved ones injured and loved ones left behind. Lord, let this be a reminder of the men and woman that choose to do Your will by helping others. They continually save lives while they risk their own. You give them courage when others are afraid. You give them strength to endure when others cannot, and You give them compassion beyond compare. Thank You for these brave men and women. I pray that we always respect those that fight for our freedom, protect our streets and face danger and death daily. Like Jesus, many of these every day heroes have given their life so others may live. God, I ask that You help us to always remain faithful and that we never forget their sacrifice and forever honor them as we do Your Son. In the precious name of Jesus, I pray. Amen.

2 Chronicles 7:14 - if my people, who are called by my name, will humble themselves and pray and seek my face and turn from their wicked ways, then I will hear from heaven, and I will forgive their sin and will heal their land.

Dear God, our Lord and Savior,

There is no time like the present to lift our nation up to You. It is no wonder our morality has suffered with the widespread failure to obey Your commandments. You have rewarded "One Nation Under God" with spiritual and material abundance yet, as a whole, we have rebelled against You and refused to live by the standards You have set forth for us. Lord, I pray that We The People, acknowledge that we depend totally on You and we need You to intervene in our country's situation. Together we must pray as a Nation for a revival of honest, capable leaders. May each of us confess our sins, repent of them, and show agreement with You that what we have done displeases You and that we should turn away from wrongdoing. May the people of the United States challenge each other to kneel before You, have faith and believe that if enough of Your children cry out to You, You will restore our country and make us into a nation that honors You again. Today, as always, Lord, I pray from my heart that all of America looks to You and cries out, confident that You desire to work on our behalf. In Jesus' name, Amen.

HAPPY FIRST DAY OF SCHOOL

Lord,

Thank you for providing our world with schools and teachers and filling our children with knowledge. May each child find joy as they discover new beginnings, and may they be thankful for the fresh start that is given with each day of school. Please help the children grow in mind and body with words of encouragement from their peers, teachers, and parents so that their hearts will be drawn to a special interest that will lead them to a bright future. May prayer and The Good Book be part of a daily routine so they may begin their days with the Words of our Savior; and may these words guide them to have the desire to learn and do well in school, to respect their teachers and classmates and to find entertainment with God-loving, God-fearing friends. Please let all be safe on the roads to and from school, during classes, and while attending sporting events. Grant wisdom and support between parents, teachers, and students so the line of communication will remain open, and cooperation with all will be reached. As parents, we are thankful for these gifts of life that You allow us to share with You. They are precious in our eyes too. In the name of Jesus. Amen.

Compliments of God

Veterans Day

Dear Lord,

     Today is a day set aside to pay tribute to those who have served our country, to express our gratitude for their courage and selfless act of protecting our homeland and fighting for our freedom. May each of us take a moment to pray that You bless them for their continual struggle to preserve our freedom, the fight for our safety, and for our country's heritage that was founded to be one nation under God. Lord I pray for those that are among us today and for generations past. Many have entered into danger, suffered wounds that may still be healing, endured separation from loved ones, been deprived of rest and sleep, worked long hours during war and peace and, for too many, contributed their own life. May You bless these men and women and their families abundantly for their devotion and courage. May we never let them down. May we always maintain the values of freedom with dignity. May we lead the world by example by showing kindness, tolerance and love toward each other. It is then that the dedication and sacrifices of our veterans will be honored not only by our words, but by our deeds. God bless America. In the name of the Holy Son, Jesus. Amen.

My brother, Bill- United States Navy-1968
Sent to me in a letter from Italy.

Fort Hood

Dear God,

    First, thank You for the many courageous men and women that serve our country every day to help keep us safe and free. Yesterday's shooting at an army base was another nightmare imposed upon our military and their families. Please be with the families and friends of those that had loved ones taken from them. May they somehow feel peace knowing that their life here on earth was not in vain. Please help the wounded heal and be whole again. Secondly, Lord, please help the men, women, and children that have experienced the tragedy of war and now suffer from the aftermath of the horrific sights and sounds. Clear their minds of any and all things remembered that will cause distress and harm to themselves or another human being. Please let them know they are safe when they return home to their country they helped defend. This land is Your Creation; our safe haven on earth. May it be harvested for the betterment of mankind; may the people honor You and do Your will with respect for one another. May we turn to the Word for comfort and peace, and may we forever trust in those Words written for us to obey. In the name of Jesus. Amen.

Dear Lord,

Today let us take the time to say a special prayer for the educational system and all the people that make it come together for our children. There are the teachers, of course, that share their knowledge, who care and sometimes pray for their students. The principals that make it all run smoothly on a day-to-day basis. The bus driver that makes sure the kids get to and from school safely; the ladies and men in the cafeteria that prepare the food for lunches, and the janitor and maintenance workers that clean and repair. There are the office employees with their daily reports of attendance, and the students that take time out of their day to help where they can. And let us not forget all the parents that volunteer and lend a helping hand. We have the freedom of education, from daycare to our last days as a senior in high school and then on to the college of our choice. Through all the levels, we have been blessed with these incredible people. Thank You for these special human beings that You created and placed in our lives. May You grant them patience, wisdom, and courage as they face each day with a challenge. Lord, please guide us to teach our children to show respect for those who have authority. May each student study the lessons assigned, gain knowledge of substance, and take it with them to share with the world. I pray that, You, the greatest Teacher of mankind, will be pleased. In Christ we pray, Amen

Memorial Day

Dear Lord,

    Every year we mark our calendars on specific days to remind us to celebrate or commemorate various events. Right now it is the end of May and with that comes much change. Spring draws to an end and summer is just around the corner, and that means school is almost out for most of the kids. Bags, along with cars, will be packed; and family vacations will soon begin. The smell of the smoking backyard BBQ's fills the air; block parties are planned; the parks are crowded with family reunions and community events; couples walk hand-in-hand or perhaps with their dog at the end of a leash, taking in the fresh air, the sight of green grass, and the sound of laughter that surrounds them. Your invitation to enjoy the lakes, rivers, and oceans are answered by our attendance as sailboats glide across the water, powered by the wind that You provide. Fisherman roll their eyes, and probably utter a few words, as the motor boats pass by; rains will fall and fill the waterways and provide the needed nourishment for our food and wildlife. There is the long-awaited warmth of the pool water that brings the sound of the spring in the diving board and the anticipation of the big splash that will follow. There are festivals on the main streets of small towns, and outside musical concerts that make us move and clap our hands, bringing back a fond memory or two; we attend the good old-fashion-fun-time traveling carnivals that were sometimes the highlight of our summer when we were kids. Large tents will start popping up in various areas with signs announcing the Christian revivals or vacation bible school. All these things are signs of the time. All these "things" are ours to enjoy because You have provided for us. TODAY, Lord, let us be reminded not only of the "things" that you provide but of Your creation of the men and women who were born to be members of our United States Army, U.S. Navy, U.S. Air Force, and United States Marine Corp.

I pray that EVERY day of the year we show our sincere thanks to these men and women by not just setting aside a day for them, but by all of us living a life that echoes the words "proud to be an American". I pray that the corruption of Your people, of our government, and the greed of the world end today. Let freedom ring, not because of the wars that are fought, or the commands of the rulers of the world, but because we live a God-loving, God-fearing life. Thank You, Lord, for Your sacrifice of Your Son and for the battle You fight each day with the demons we possess. Thank You for the American soldier, for Your creation we call the United States of America, and for the freedom that allows us to love You. In honor of the lives that were sacrificed for us and for the sacrifice of Your Son, Jesus, I say thank You. Amen.

Heavenly Father,

You are the founding Father of all nations. Please raise all nations up to care and serve the people that dwell in their boundaries. I have been blessed with a life in a land of FREEDOM and unlimited opportunity. Thank You for the freedom to worship You. God, I pray that You raise up the Christian voice so it may be heard by our leaders of this once-great nation and cause us, as Believers, to become the standard bearers to such a degree that we can profoundly affect the morality of this nation. Endow with the Spirit of wisdom those to whom in Your Name we entrust the authority of government, that there may be justice and peace at home; and that, through obedience to Your law, we may show forth Your praise among the nations on earth. May we as a nation of Christians, Catholics and Protestants, turn our hearts to You and open our eyes to the error of our ways and form a united front against the wickedness of the devil.

Protect us from the evil that lurks from within and from without. Inspire in all of us the desire to do Your Will and only Your Will. May Your touch open our creative spirit, our growth as a nation, and our unlimited hope for the future.

In time of prosperity fill our hearts with thankfulness, and in the day of trouble do not allow our trust in You to fail. May we always be ONE NATION UNDER GOD. In the name of Jesus Christ, Amen.

Compliments of God

Dear Lord,

    I know that praying for our pastor and those that minister to others in Your name, is very important. I hope that all Christians come together in prayer, on a daily basis and pray for the pastors of the world, church leaders and those that give their time in missionary work. May they remain faithful to You and their commitments as they embrace the gifts and talents that You have given them. Please watch over them and keep them safe from harm; give them rest after their long days of work and provide them with food for strength and good health. I pray they always turn to You for direction so they will expand their knowledge and wisdom to continue the pattern of sound teaching. You have qualified them to preach the Word to all who surround them. May they never abuse this privilege. As Your children, may we support the church by giving our time to help; and may we encourage others to do the same. Lord, I lift up all ministers of God in prayer today as they express their love for You by sharing Your word and giving all glory to You. In the name of Your Son, Jesus, Amen.

Never Forget

It was about 8:30 AM and I was coming back from dropping my dog off at the groomer. I had returned from Seattle the day before and I was still very tired from the long "non-stop" weekend. As I drove toward the house, the day ahead ran through my mind. I was tired and successful in talking myself out of my usual morning workout. The past weekend events brought a smile to my face as I reminisced of the fun I had with my friends in Washington. My thoughts quickly switched to what I might wear that day since I had dinner plans that evening after work. As I pulled into the driveway of my house, my thoughts were interrupted by a break in the music on the radio. The local DJ reported that a plane had hit one of the World Trade Centers in New York City. My first thought was how could that be; how could a pilot be that careless? Still caught up in my own world, I continued to move about with my daily planning. Not breaking routine, I clicked the TV on to listen to my favorite morning show while I got ready for work. What I saw, what I heard and what followed will forever be embedded in my mind.

Dear Lord,

September 11, 2001. Lord, I pray that we never forget the men and women that lost their lives that day simply by following their daily routine. I am sure the thoughts that ran through their mind the morning of 9-11 were similar to the ones I had the same morning. Was it the kid's play at school that day; or the dog that needed to be groomed; their dinner plans after work or maybe it was just a day to skip that exhausting morning workout? Whatever their last thoughts were, nothing had prepared them or this nation for the events that occurred that horrid day, 13 years ago. As a nation we came together. People of all religions, political parties and race were united in a stand against the terror that had struck our country. We held our loved ones closer, we shared our thoughts with each other, even strangers; we volunteered our time and we gave money to help our country. We turned to You and mostly we prayed. Lord, today, my request is simple. Today, I pray that each of Your children, the world over, honor the loved ones lost by honoring You. With renewed faith, may we all return to the power of prayer. In the name of the Son of God, Jesus, I pray. Amen.

In memory of the victims of 9-11

Ground Zero- New York City, NY

Julo Spencer

Family And Friends

Father's Day

Dear God,

  Today on Father's Day may we honor and praise the fathers that strive to balance the demands of work, marriage and fatherhood. They are our first teachers, our role models, our heroes. May we recognize their honest awareness of both joy and sacrifice. I pray that You will give them strength to be moral leaders so they will be shining examples to their sons and daughters. God please bless the man that, despite divorce, has remained in his children's lives. Bless the step-father who so freely chose the obligation of fatherhood. Bless the fathers who have lost a child to death and continue to hold the child in their heart. Let us pray for the fathers who have been hurt by neglect or hostility of their children. Let us praise the fathers who have died but live on in our memory. Thank you Father for Your love and grace that continues to nurture us. And thank You for making our hearts smile. In Your Son's name, we pray. Amen.

  Happy Father's Day

Compliments of God

Matthew 7:7 "Ask and it will be given to you; seek and you will find; knock and the door will be opened to you." (NIV).

Be Careful What You Pray For

More than once, this verse has come to play in my life. I pray for this, that, or another, and it appears that God has ignored me and does not answer my prayers. But, never fear, at some point, in some way, He does. I have learned to be careful what I pray for.

My step-father, Tom, was diagnosed with colon cancer in the spring of '94. He had surgery within a couple of weeks of the diagnosis; and, unfortunately, with that came many complications. Tom went home from the hospital with all of us thinking the surgery had been a success. Within days of his operation, infection set in and a second surgery was needed. Unbeknownst to the surgeon, a bowel was punctured during the first surgery. Because the puncture had gone undetected, and the infection severe, there was a lot of damage done. The doctors warned us that they may not be able to save him. The first 48 hours after his second operation were, as always in situations as this, very critical. We prayed hard for him to pull through this; and, thankfully, he did. God had answered our prayers. However, the diagnosis was not by any means what we wanted to hear. The healing process was going to be extensive and treatments would be very aggressive; still with only a chance of survival for three to five more years. Regardless, we were thankful for the time we had been given.

Days turned into weeks and weeks into months of Tom's constant fight to survive. He was being fed through an IV and had lost over 100 pounds. There were bouts of dropped blood pressure causing trips in and out of ICU. He contracted numerous staph infections that would put him under quarantine. The twice-daily visits, along with the scare calls to come to the hospital, took a toll on my mom. I could see the worry, the sadness, and the fatigue in her face and eyes. I prayed for God to give her strength. I prayed for my dad to heal and come home.

December rolled around and Tom was easing up on the six-month anniversary of his hospital stay. Although tired from all he had been through, his spirits were beginning to rise. The visits were more of laughter and actual conversations now; no more just watching him sleep while holding his hand. No more ups and downs with his vital signs, and no more trips in the middle of the night after a distress call from the hospital. The day came that he was taken off of the IV and was able to eat solid food. They started with the soft stuff first…pudding, gelatin and clear liquids. He did well. The future looked bright for our holidays together. I thanked God for our time with my dad and prayed He would let him be home for Christmas.

Christmas Day was getting close, but even with Tom's strong improvement the doctors thought it was best he stay in the hospital. Mom and I decorated his room with the usual red and green colors. I brought in a very small tree, complete with festive ornaments and the twinkling mini-lights that my dad so enjoyed watching. We placed a few small gifts under it, and smiled as we watched him grin like a child. We all chuckled when he asked if there was a hamburger in one of the boxes. I could see it was going to be our best Christmas ever together.

On December 22nd, just days before Christmas Day, the doctor allowed Tom to eat some real food. The request for a hamburger was granted, and we all celebrated with him as he took the first bite. Life was good!

Much later that night, after having dinner with some friends, I went by the hospital just to check on Tom. When I arrived, things were not right. He was hallucinating, talking crazy, and talking to me like I was mom. I was told by the nurse on duty that there was nothing to be concerned with, and it was normal behavior from the meds. Reluctantly, dismissing my concerns, I went home for the night.

Early the next morning, December 23rd, I received a call from Tom's doctor requesting that I bring my mother to the hospital. Tom had been moved back to ICU and was on life support. The family gathered together, along with many friends, to help support our last cries to God for a miracle. Hours passed before the doctor told us there was nothing more they could do for my dear Daddy Tom. They took him off of life support and moved him to a room in which he would be comfortable and would accommodate the family and friends. The early morning soon turned into afternoon, then into evening. As nightfall approached Tom was still breathing on his own. If only for a while, we found this to be promising.

As the night of the 23rd began to come to a close, Tom's breathing was more faint and his breaths further and further apart. We knew his time with us was nearing an end. I remember my mother holding his hand as she looked up at me and my brothers and said, "I'm losing my best friend".

Growing up our family gift exchange was always celebrated on Christmas Eve rather than Christmas morning, as tradition knows it. It was momma's tradition, and it was something that each of her children respected and followed for her.

The sadness of my dad leaving this earth, and missing him always, is difficult even to this day. I used to ask myself if I prayed for the wrong thing. Did I pray selfishly for my dad to live so I would be happy? Maybe. It never once crossed my mind that my prayer to bring Tom home for the holidays would be answered as it was. My meaning was to let him heal, get well, and be at the house with my mother so we could do our traditional Christmas Eve celebrating. Never doubting or questioning, I know that God knew what I meant; and, in His divine plan, He answered my prayer.

Just minutes after midnight, Christmas Eve, on the day we planned our celebration, Tom let go. He had gone Home for Christmas.

I find nothing wrong in asking for someone to be healed (or anything specific for that matter); but remember, my friends, be prepared for the answer. It will come. God's plan includes every breath we take. Be careful what you pray for.

Compliments of God

Daddy Tom – January 7, 1938 – December 24, 1994

Lord,

Like many of Your children, You have brought much joy into my life by blessing me with wonderful, loyal, and God-loving friends. We have shared tears of sorrow and tears of joy. We have laughed out loud at each other and even louder at ourselves. We spend time together; we share our families and friends with each other; and above all, we share our love for You, with everyone. I pray that whoever is reading this devotional will stop and thank You, right now, for that special friend that is in their life. Thank You for the special people in my life. In Jesus name I pray. Amen.

Dear God,

    I have been blessed with a specific set of people in my life that to Your purpose, complete me. Thank you for my friends who are truly friends, for my soul mate, and, for my brothers and sisters in Christ. I pray now for those who do not have a special person to complete their lives. Please send the right person to those in need; one to offer encouragement, friendship, loving guidance, and unconditional love; one that will just be there. I pray that a bond of Christian love will develop and that both people will be uplifted. Please forgive me for not always letting my special people know how much they mean, and help me to show them their importance in my life. I praise You and thank You for always being there for me, too. And for Your promise to never leave nor forsake me. In Jesus' name I pray. Amen.

A good night wish to my friends

May you rest well tonight in knowing that God's grace will watch over you as you slumber. Worry not; only dream of all the God-given blessings that have been bestowed upon you, giving Glory to God for providing the light over all of your life. Sweet dreams!

Dear God,

    My prayers today are with all parents, grandparents that may be raising kids, or foster parents that are trying so desperately to help a child in need. Sometimes they struggle to raise decent, respectful children. Over time there has been a slow erosion of mannerly children. It has brought us to a situation today where the lack of respect that many kids show their parents, their teachers, one another and even strangers is astounding and disturbing. Please help us as role models to teach our children not to be rude and disrespectful. Let us not worry about being the cool parent, allowing them to make their own choices at a young age and expecting good results. Instead let us pray with our kids, teach our kids to say "please" and "thank you", lead by example and to always show love and affection in all circumstances. Teach us to be better parents so that our children will have hearts of gratitude and concern for others and not a disposition of selfishness and entitlement. Lord I pray that You take our hand and lead us so that we may lead our children to a better, happier and more productive life. May we set the bar high and live the life You want for our children; a life of respect that will be a blessing to everyone that comes into contact with them. Above all may we as Christian parents teach them to know You so that someday when they have children of their own, You will take their hand and they too will follow Your lead. In the name of Jesus, Your Son. Amen.

Dear Lord,

Bless my friends and family with the energy to refuel their minds and bodies with Your word.

When we are hungry we feed our bodies with food; when our car is empty we stop and fill the tank. I pray that we all do the same for our bodies when we are drained emotionally and spiritually. I pray that each of us finds our solitary place each day and that we spend time in prayer and focus solely on You to refuel our minds, body and spirit.

"Very early in the morning, while it was still dark, Jesus got up, left the house and went off to a solitary place where he prayed" (Mark 1:35-36).

May we each have the discipline to honor Jesus' example so that we may have full victory and power in our Christian walk. Thank You Lord for our daily strength that You give us to follow Your Son. In the name of Jesus I pray and say GLORY TO GOD. Amen.

Good morning Lord,

Today I am thinking of all the children at church camp this summer. Thank you for giving them this opportunity to know You better and grow closer to You. May this be for the children who already know You, a time to strengthen their relationship. And for those children who are coming to know You for the first time, come to build a strong, lasting and loving relationship with You. There will be thousands of kids in camp who will get to experience You through nature, the teachers, and challenging outdoor activities. May those teachings be a success and may none of the children get hurt.

Lord I also pray for the teachers during their class time. I ask that they are able to change the life of each child there with the Word of God; that the kids behave properly and learn how to shine with Christ's Light in this dark world.

May the children be obedient to the Holy Spirit and acquire the tools to use against peer pressure of all kinds. May they learn to share the words and teachings of the Bible outside of the classroom and services and acknowledge that hearts can be changed.

Above all may they know and understand that "Jesus loves the little children. All the children of the world…red and yellow, black and white, they are precious in His sight, Jesus loves the little children of the world." Lord, let them learn to put away all prejudices and see each other as You do. For these things I thank You and pray in Your Son's name. Amen.

Julo Spencer

Dear God,

    Today family and friends will gather to help celebrate my husband's "first" 50 years on earth. Thank you for sending him to me and letting me share his life with him. He is my soul mate, my saint, hero and the love of my life and I ask that you give him many more healthy years here in this beautiful world You created. Thank you for letting family arrive safely last night and for all the help they are giving me to prepare for our big celebration tonight. May You provide safety to the other family members and friends that will be driving to and from our house today. May we all behave responsibly as You would expect us to. Thank you Lord as always for providing all our needs. Amen.

"The hubby"

Dear Lord,

You have given so many men and women the awesome opportunity of parenthood. I pray for the parents of every child that they will ask You for wisdom to raise their children and to lead by example. May they not be passive, but aggressive with their teachings of right and wrong; teach that lying is wrong, drugs and alcohol abuse is wrong, cheating, stealing, and impurity is wrong. May they all guide their sons and daughters to a Godly life, using the Bible as reference when an issue arises. Lord, I pray for adults who have abused or neglected their children and ask that You help them with their faith and grant grace and mercy to them. Please show these mothers and fathers, You are the Great I Am and will save them from a life of unhappiness and struggle if they will only believe in You and turn to You in their time of need and frustration. May they all come to know their Savior and speak to Him from their hearts and not just their mouths. God, I know You love all of us as Your own children. Please help the parents, present and future, show their children the same Love. Thank you God for hearing our prayers. In the name of the Son of God, Jesus, we pray. Amen

Heavenly Father,

Today I pray for a child caring for a parent that once cared for them. Though this time of role reversal can be somewhat rewarding, it can also be stressful and draining. Please provide balance with work and marriage; energy in caring for their children and household; patience, compassion and a sense of humor when caring for their parent. I ask that You grant the caregiver the understanding of what an elderly mom or dad may be experiencing with their frustration of not being able to care for one's self; the roller coaster of emotions they go through or the physical pain and immobility they may have, caused by their decline in health. And may the parent understand the love that this child is showing by giving so much of their time away from others and their own needs. Grant harmony and reflection for both the mother or father and the child so all will come to treasure this time together and appreciate the sacrifices that have been made. Above all may both practice the tender love for each other that You give us on a daily basis. May there be no other time in their lives that shows a greater love for each other that what they have in the here and now. I pray that each of us follows through with the mission you have entrusted to us. Please come and prepare our hearts for a new experience of unconditional love so we will always show courage and self-sacrifice and recognize the need to show compassion, tenderness, gentleness, patience and deep gratitude. Thank you Lord. In the name of Jesus Christ. Amen.

Children, obey your parents in the Lord, for this is right. "Honor your father and mother" (this is the first commandment with a promise), "that it may go well with you and that you may live long in the land." Fathers, do not provoke your children to anger, but bring them up in the discipline and instruction of the Lord. Ephesians 6:1-4

Good morning God,

    Lord, please teach all of us that it is okay to discipline our children. In fact, Your Word tells us to do so. Thank You Lord for giving us free will but forgive us of the inclination to sin against You. We all need discipline so we can learn how to bring our desires in line with Your plan and purpose for our lives. Please give us this much- needed discipline so we may gratify You for the lessons to be learned. In the same way, teach us and give us strength and knowledge to discipline our children. May we follow Your ways in disciplining out of love and not anger and may our children understand this is the way of our Lord. Let us teach them to submit to authority so they will receive Your love and blessings. And from this love and these blessings may they also pass discipline to their children in a way that pleases You. Thank You God for hearing our prayers. May all glory be to You. Amen.

I SAID YES

My husband and I pretty much knew that within weeks of knowing each other that we would spend the rest of our lives together, although it would not be openly mentioned for several more months. We both agreed on what we called our Two Year Plan; not discussing marriage until we knew each other for at least two years. We stayed true to our plan...for the most part.

As a couple, we entertained a lot; inviting family members and friends so the two worlds would hopefully mesh. We hosted backyard barbecues, fish fries, birthday parties, and an annual wine tasting party that usually kicked off the holiday season. With the size of Duncan's family, there was always something going on. Everyone got together for the kids' birthdays, special anniversaries, or events for well-earned accomplishments by one family member or another. The week of the Fourth of July was an annual get together at the family lake house. Thanksgiving Day was at his sister's house, and Christmas was celebrated early in December with the entire family on his mother's side. It was any excuse to get together as a family; and that was just fine with me. Family orientation was one of the many things I found attractive about my relationship with Duncan. Growing up, it was something I always wished for with my family.

About a year and a half after our first date Duncan and I, along with his sister and her husband, decided it would be fun to vacation in the wine country of California.

It was a milestone birthday for Duncan, so the trip was my gift to him. Duncan's younger brother, who lived in San Francisco and was quite familiar with the places to tour, joined us. The scenery was beautiful and peaceful. The vineyards were as green as you will ever see them. The plump grapes, dressed in their little jackets of reds, greens and purples, ready for harvesting, hung from the vines; their colors so vivid they would trump any box of crayons. Wineries with buildings mirroring Tuscany, as if they were staged for a painter's canvas; and if you used your imagination while driving on the highway along the Pacific, one could almost envision the Amalfi coast of Italy. It is one of my fondest memories.

But as all good things, our time in California was drawing to a close. We had only one more day to enjoy the beauty of the western part of the country and the relief of the Texas heat. Being our last day, Duncan and I decided to spend it together; just the two of us. We drove south of the city along the coast on Hwy. 1 enjoying the sight of the sapphire blue waters of the Pacific. The waves, raged at times, roaring and hitting the rocky edges of the cliffs that line the Big Sur area. We lunched in Monterrey, then continued on our journey just a few miles away to Carmel By The Sea; one of the most beautiful, quaint, and romantic little cities I have ever been to. We strolled up and down the streets, stopping only to admire something that caught our eye in a window of one of the many locally owned stores. We both commented on the number of small but lovely hotels that intertwined with the shops and bistros and talked of plans to come back someday when we had more time. As we neared the end of the street, I prepared myself to cross over and make our way back to the car. But, to my surprise, Duncan grabbed my hand and led me through the doorway of the last jewelry store on Main St. The expression on my face was of confusion, yet on the inside I have to admit I was a bit excited. He smiled and said, "We are just looking". And that's exactly what we did.

The beach is just a few hundred feet from the center of town, so we decided to venture down there. Carrying our shoes, we walked along the sands hand in hand listening to the ocean in our own silence as if we both knew that no words between us were needed. One has to know this is the perfect time and place for a proposal. Not totally surprised, the matter of marriage did not come up. And, honestly, as giddy as I was with the thought that Duncan might pop the question, I was not quite ready to make the commitment. The time was just not right for either of us. After all, the day of the two-year agreement was not here yet.

The warm days of summer were easing their way out, and the cool mornings and evenings of autumn were moving in. We began to make plans for the holidays, as we both made sure our schedules of work and family would coincide with our time together. Thanksgiving Day is a big deal to Duncan's sister (her favorite holiday) so it was a sure thing that we would spend it at her house.

That day came and with Duncan's son Gunnar in tow, we headed to Austin for dinner with his family and friends. Attendance that year was good. Mothers, dads, in-laws and out-laws were there; brothers had arrived from out of town with their mates; cousins from just down the street, and friends from neighboring cities. All there to enjoy the feast and, much to the hostess' liking, the perfect way to celebrate her favorite holiday.

As the day came to a close and most of the friends started heading out the door, the family lingered. It was a rare occasion that all the siblings in Duncan's family were together, so Duncan suggested that we take a family photo. As I powdered my nose and brushed my hair, I could hear the family gathering in the other room and I was summoned to hurry and get in there. But when I entered the room, something was a bit amiss. The majority of the family was on one side, while Duncan and Gunnar were on the other. I knew immediately what was about to happen. I gasped and covered my face to hide the tears that were trying to leak out of my eyes. The family was confused; questions began to fly out of everyone's mouth as the crowd got louder. With Gunnar standing between us, Duncan began to speak. It is all kind of fuzzy to me, but I do remember Duncan's first words were "as everyone knows"...it's a bit more of a blur to me exactly what came next. I gathered my thoughts and composed myself long enough to see Gunnar look up at me and say, "dad wants you to marry us". He handed me a small box. I took the ring from the box and gave it to Gunnar, and he placed it on my hand. As I hugged him tightly, I looked up at Duncan to see tears in his eyes. I joked with him and said our two years was not up; but 30 days before the deadline, was close enough for him (and me). Six months to the day, with Gunnar by his dad's side as the "best" best man, we were married in the backyard of what would become our home together. The rest is history.

A man's greatest treasure is his wife. She is a gift from the Lord. Proverbs 18:22

Heavenly Father,

    Thank You for creating the institution of marriage; bringing two people together as one. The union of man and woman is a precious gift that should be taken seriously. May each husband cherish, protect and provide for his wife as You have instructed. May each wife love and honor her husband. And may there be a mutual respect for one another. Together may they surround themselves with the Words of Your teachings, making You the center of their lives so that everything will fall into place and their life together will be full of blessings from above. May there be loving words spoken and may each heart be filled with understanding and forgiveness. I ask that we learn to trust and to continually increase our faith in You. Bless all marriages with peace and happiness and let Your love be our guiding light for Your glory and our peace and joy not only here but in eternity. With praise to You, our Lord. Amen.

Compliments of God

Dear Lord,

Ten years ago today you blessed me with a man I call my best friend. We know marriage takes work, but You have walked with us every step of the way, keeping our trust strong, and bringing out the best in each other. We have faced sorrows together and worked through conflicts together. We have experienced adventures, fun times, and laughter. We have sound family ties and, together, have gained the blessing of many wonderful friends. Lord, thank You for bringing this Christian man into my life. His Faith and love never ceases to amaze me. Please forgive me of the times I have been selfish and inconsiderate, difficult to live with, and for the times I failed to give needed understanding. I pray that You will continue to walk with us and inspire us to lead Christian lives. May we always have a true and understanding love for each other, filled with faith and trust. May we bear with one another's weaknesses and grow from each other's strengths. May nothing ever divide us. I pray the love that brought us together grows and matures with each passing year, and may that love bring us both ever closer to You. Let us always find peace in knowing that You will lead us to unending happiness in Heaven. In the name of our Father's Son, Jesus, Amen.

Compliments of God

Julo Spencer

Lord,

    Thank you for creating Gunnar, and for placing him in my life. There have been ups and downs in our relationship as parent and child but there has been no greater joy in my life than to watch this child laugh and have fun with family and friends over the years. May the fun times and awesome experiences continue for him in the years to come. With each year that passes may he learn to do justly and to walk with You in obedience. As children lose their innocence at a younger and younger age these days, I pray that Gunnar uses good judgment and practices high morals with his choices as a young man. I ask that Gunnar glorify You in his heart as he discovers the talents and abilities You have given to him, as his will becomes stronger with age. I pray that his knowledge of the Word and the scriptures of the Bible continues to increase with maturity. Please grant him compassion, love, respect, self-control and self-discipline when matters arise. As he turns 16 years old today, I pray that our relationship grows to be stronger, more trusting and forever loving toward each other. Gunnar is a gift from You, and I thank You, God, for blessing me with this young man. In Jesus name I pray, Amen.

Happy birthday Gunnar

Compliments of God

Dear Father in Heaven,

Thank You for the friends, family, even strangers that bring laughter to our life. You have given us a sense of humor so we may enjoy the funny side of everyday situations. Your great unending love gives us inspiration and a spirit of imagination and creativity. Please help us to use that spirit to play more and to laugh more.

Remind us that laughter is truly the best medicine. It has no bad side effects, you don't need a prescription, and it doesn't cost a cent; it's God given. We laugh out loud and it heals the wounds within us; we laugh until we cry which brings tears of joy to our eyes; we laugh until our sides hurt, we laugh at others; and, hopefully, we can all laugh at ourselves.

Thank You for the laughter with friends that helps our bond grow stronger, for the laughter of children that brings heart-warming pleasure to our life, and for the silliness and laughter that only family can understand and enjoy. God I know that everyone has days that are challenging and most stressful, and those days can easily drain us of life's little pleasures. I pray for those who cannot find their laughter today. But for those of us who can, and will, may we look up to You and with joy in our hearts, say Thank You for bringing this smile to my face. Amen.

Dear Lord,

    Tomorrow someone near and dear to my heart will be baptized. Thank You for giving him the chance to redeem himself and be cleansed from sin. May he feel You in his heart and know that this sacramental action is his commitment to You; to follow You and do good works in Your honor and glory. You are our merciful God and Father of our children. As all good children may we obey Your commands as You fulfill the Promise with Your unfailing love. May my friend receive the fullness of Your grace; his sins be washed away and may he understand that without these blessings no one can enter the Kingdom of God. May he increase his knowledge and strengthen his faith. May there be no doubt that You are the only way and that life is beautiful with You in it. I pray that he is never ashamed or denies You. May he always lift his head high with love from deep within his soul and say YOU ARE MY GOD. YOU ARE THE WAY. YOU ARE ETERNAL LIFE. May he be Yours forever. In Jesus' name, Amen.

Compliments of God

Brant- October 5, 2013

Dear Father in Heaven,

No family is perfect. We argue, we disagree on a number of issues, we may even worship differently; and, far too often, we stop speaking to each other. In reality one family member, be it brother, sister, father, mother or child is no more to blame than the other. God please let all family members be aware of what they are doing to each other. May each understand that as adult children, brothers or sisters, we live individual lives that may not coincide with the way the others may live. We will honor our mothers and fathers, but please let them realize that they are not in control. Children break away and what they consider to be right and wrong, how they raise their own children or perhaps how their time is spent with family as a whole may differ from other family member's opinions. You and only You are the Judge. If there has been a disagreement, a misunderstanding between siblings, children or parents, please may everyone find forgiveness in their hearts so the hurt will be healed or the anger will subside. Lord, may You be so kind as to give us the unity, peace and mutual love that You found in Your own family. May the head of each family obtain strength and wisdom. Father I ask that you bless the children in our families. Help them to be obedient and devoted to their parents so they will be more like You. May they grow in wisdom and age and grace before You and man. Help all of us to be pure and kind, gentle and self-sacrificing. May pride be set aside so forgiveness and love will take over. Give us passion for our God intended roles within family. In the end, family is family and we are blessed. Thank You for blessing me with my siblings, my son, my husband and my extended family. As an individual may my family, and even those around me, reap a great benefit from my faith in You. Lord I pray that each of us looks to You and, in prayer, ask that You make our family and home more and more like Yours, until we are all ONE family, happy and at peace in our true Home with You. Thank You Father. In the name of Your loving Son, Jesus. Amen.

Dear Lord,

Thank You for the people You have introduced me to while on my journey. Thank You for the acquaintances that offered wise words or a smile. Thank You for the childhood friends that provided so many fun days in the neighborhood I grew up in. Thank You especially for the classmates that were kind and inspiring; the class clowns that made me laugh; for the besties that passed notes in the hallway; guys in the bands that I had a secret crush on; for the Homecoming Queen that smiled and made me feel special; for the pretty blonde with the prefect hair that I admired so; for the boy that gave me my first kiss; even the bully's that only made me stronger. Lord, I know that each one of these people was a blessing from You; each one with a purpose that gave me moments in my life that will never be mine again. Thank You for letting me reconnect with a few of them. May the journey continue with a new purpose, new moments and new blessings. And for those of them that have come Home to be with You, may their memories live on forever. In Jesus name. Amen. SHHS'71

February 10

Lord,

    I reach out today in prayer and ask that You, our Father of compassion, help my friends and their family members, who are grieving with a loss that they may have suffered, past or present. May You walk with them today and touch them in such a way that they will feel Your unfailing love and kindness deep within their souls. You are their God of hope. Please fill them with peace so they may sense the presence of Your love. May any anger or disappointment be replaced with joy and understanding. May the pain and sorrow be lifted and replaced with peace and strength. Thank You for closing out the darkness with the light that only You can provide. Please guide each of us to embrace the days ahead with certainty that NOTHING can destroy the GOOD that has been given. In the loving name of Jesus. Amen.

Proverbs 23:22 Listen to your father who gave you life, and do not despise your mother when she is old.

Dear Father in Heaven,

I hear many mothers and fathers talk about their children with pride. They have done their best to raise their sons and daughters to be respectful, well-mannered, and happy as they grow into adulthood. We tend to overindulge and spoil our kids today with whatever they want. It seems the words "thank you" or "pleased to meet you" have all become words of another generation. Lord, I pray that parents bring back the family values that help make the world today what You want it to be. As our children prepare to embark on a new life as an adult with visions of education, careers, and families on the horizon, may they not overindulge their children but let them learn from the true teachings of the Bible by wanting little and giving a lot. May parents be respected and looked upon as mentors rather than rulers. May we be parents first, friends second. May all hearts be touched with compassion as each family member ages. Please let eyes be open to the time, effort, and love that has been bestowed upon a child's life. May these children realize that as their parents approach the golden years that it is their duty, their calling, to become the adult and care for a sick parent, to remember them on special days throughout the year, and to love them unconditionally. May both sides express respect and show love with each conversation or discussion. Give parents the insight to know that as their children become adults that they need to cut them loose and let them grow into the people that You want them to be. May they advise a son or daughter; but let that child make their own choices rather than what is wanted of, or for them. May all who believe know that You are in control. Above all, I pray that every father, mother, son, and daughter will look to You as the center of their family and experience the spiritual union. May You be glorified and pleased, and may all families be blessed. In Jesus name I pray. Amen.

Proverbs 22:6 Train up a child in the way he should go; even when he is old he will not depart from it.

April 9, 2014

Dear Lord,

    We know that loss is an ongoing part of life. May You be near the broken hearted as they mourn the sudden loss of a friend and father. An acquaintance to some, a legend to others, but for many he was a true friend that brought fun and laughter to their lives; a fighter and warrior in and out of the ring. Lord, may all who still remain on this earth understand and cope with their sudden loss. There are challenges ahead with an array of feelings; none of them wrong. I ask that the time of unprepared grief not overwhelm but be gradually absorbed with the reality of this loss and how life will change without him. God, I pray for this man's children today that they will find forgiveness where needed and understanding in the shock and confusion they are experiencing. Please hold their hands through this time of sadness and let them not question "why" but understand that with You all things have purpose. Please give them strength to cope and rid them of any uncertainness for the future so they may go on living a purposeful, meaningful, and Godly life. And, Lord, though no one is ever ready to say goodbye, may we take to heart the Promise You have made to those who believe in You that heaven is a real place. May You, and only You, be the Judge. I ask in the name of the Son of God, Jesus, may our friend rest in peace. Amen.

Dear God,

    Today I come to you with a broken heart with news of a friend. Please be with her and the family during this time of sadness for all of them. And while You are at it, please watch over a few others I know who need You right now, too; maybe more than ever. I pray for their family members that are ill and the loved ones by their side taking care of them the best they can; looking to You for answers and peace. I pray for the family that recently lost their son in an accident, and my friend who is feeling selfishness and confusion at the moment. She, alone, has been through more than most of us. For our classmate who lost his sister yesterday. I am thankful he is a man of God and can find comfort in knowing You. There is no answer to illness, hard times, or loss other than it is Your way. Your way and Your timing is what we must believe is the best for everyone. Thank You, Lord, for hearing our prayers, our needs, and our wants. May we forever be grateful for the grace and mercy You grant us. In the name of Jesus, I pray. Amen.

Letting Go

Dear Father,

    My heart is heavy today as the days of being a parent are being tested strongly. Why is it so difficult to help raise a child? Certainly there is a time to let go and let our children make their own decisions, whether it be with a career and just how far to take one's education; or to let go and let them choose their own friends or try not to influence them with their choice of a lifelong mate. The hardest is allowing ourselves to "let go" as we watch them make their own mistakes. No matter the age, it is a tough job being a parent. There is no misunderstanding of the joy our child has brought to us. The giggling sound of him as a small child filling the room is one of my fondest. We had the times of our lives watching him doing simple things like running through the sprinkler during the summer, screaming from the coldness of the water only to run though it again…and again! The snowballs fights in the winter and that look of "fun fright" as the wad of snow would head towards him; the Christmas mornings and birthday parties that made his eyes light up like an airport runway; the straight "A" report cards; the first homecoming and the first date. The little-boy hugs and the cuddles, and the awe in his eyes when he realized just how much we love him. We have years of memories scrapbooked and chronicled; framed photos fill the hallways, shelves, and night tables all displaying family ties, laughter, and happiness. All wonderful memories for each of us.

As the years go by and he begins to develop a strong mind of his own, all that we have taught him about life is abruptly placed in File 13. His innocence has been replaced with attitude, his love with despise, and the stubbornness of being "right" rather than happy has taken over. I have said to my husband many times during the child-rearing years that we must do our best with our teaching skills as parents so that he will know right from wrong, to love him unconditionally and hope he learns to do the same; to share, to give, and to pray and thank God for all we have been blessed with. In our home office we have a stone that reads "Prepare the child for the path, not the path for the child." There is so much truth to that statement and, believe me, there have been many struggles with our walk to get there. But through it all, we are, and always will be, here for our son. The good, the bad, and the ugly.

Now, as this boy is on the brink of becoming a young man we find each of us fighting to stay afloat with strong wills in all corners. We now face the resistance for him to remain our child versus the resistance to let him go. In my heart, I do not believe it is time to let go just yet. He is still just a child (even though he doesn't think so) and the guidance, obedience, and stronghold of being a parent must remain intact for a little while longer. This is a tough stage of life for him as well as his dad and me. I have prayed in silence today for this little boy, this child, this teenager, this young man, in hope that he will find some understanding of how it is for us, being parents to him; and how his time will come, all too soon, to be the responsible one who will make critical decisions in his life. I pray that he understands that he is not ready for the world, as we know it, and that we are not ready to let him go.

He once wrote in a poem that contained something to this effect: "Life is like the Texas weather, if you don't like it stick around, it'll change." I hope and pray that he lives by that philosophy now and for the rest of his life. I pray he knows just how much we love him!

I was once close to my step-son. When he was a small boy we did a lot of things together. We worked on school projects together, I volunteered at his school, and we even cooked together. Trips were planned, fabulous birthday parties, and a lot of carpooling for him and his friends took place. It was always me he came to when he was not feeling well, and it was my Beef Stroganoff that he loved and requested often. Now, years gone by, he has grown up and grown away from me. We do not see eye to eye, there are no more outings together, and no more sweet chats over his favorite foods. I miss that child; but, as any parent must do, I too must accept and let go.

I was happy to hear he had befriended someone that is from a Christian upbringing and very much involved with his church family. He invited Gunnar to attend summer church camp with him and, happily, we let him go. I placed a letter in his suitcase just before he left in hopes that he would read it soon after he arrived and was settled in to camp. It was written with much meaning from my heart. I hope he keeps it and refers back to it from time to time.

Good day Gunnar,

I hope this finds you well and settled into your new digs for the week.

I read that it is highly recommended that the parents write a letter to their child while away at camp. I was happy to know this as I think this letter is long overdue from me to you.

You and I have had talks before; some were good and informative about one thing or another and others that did not go so well. I know I scold you for various reasons; for things you've done or things you haven't done that I wanted you to. You know times like that are just part of the parent/child relationship. By choice I am your step-mom, but if it makes it easier for you to understand this letter then put the step-mother/step-son thing aside for a moment and take to heart these words written especially for you. Please know that this is composed with true sincerity from my heart to yours.

I was single for eight years before I met your dad. It was somewhat of a rule of mine to not date anyone who had children. I did not want to get attached to a child only to end a relationship with the father and abandon the child; especially a child I had bonded with. But when I met your dad, something told me this time was different; and, happily, I can say I was right.

I was a teenager when my mother married my stepfather. Like most bratty kids I was determined not to like him. He was not my dad, and I didn't want him in our house acting like he was. But in a short time, I realized that he was, in fact, a very good dad to have around. He was kind hearted, honorable, God fearing; and he displayed unconditional love to me and my mom until the day he died, Christmas Eve, 1994. He was one of the most influential men in my life. He taught me so much, and I credit him for helping me be the person I am today. Our relationship was as dad and daughter, and when I moved away from home I took a piece of his heart with me. He loved me as his own, and I will be forever grateful for the time and effort he spent in making sure my life was as it should be. His name was Tom, but he was "Daddy Tom" to me. He died when he was just 58 years old, and I cried for two weeks. I still, to this day, think of him often and wish he was around to meet you and your dad. You would have loved him, too, and he would have returned that love to you and dad tenfold. I told my mother before she died in 1999 that I would never remarry unless I could find a man just like Tom to spend the rest of my life with. Well, with the patience that God gave me and by His grace, I met your dad and I knew he was "my Tom". I saw the good in him right off the bat. He's a little uptight about things, I know; but, overall, the guy is absolutely one of the most honorable men I have ever met. He, too, is kind hearted, loves you and me unconditionally, and his faith in God is unmeasurable.

I can see so much of him in you, which I am pretty sure is a good thing. Like my Daddy Tom was to me, your dad is a blessing in your life. He's a good man, and you should always honor and love him as our Lord wants you to. Make the most of your time together as the years will pass faster than you can imagine. Treasure the hunts together, the talks, the projects worked on; and the times you can laugh at, and with, one another. They are precious times that will live on in your mind for the rest of your life.

I truly believe that everything happens for a reason. I believe in God's plan, and that He looks down and laughs at all of us for trying to make our own. There is no doubt in my mind that it was God's plan that put me, you, and your dad in each other's life. He had a reason. Maybe He gave me the two of you to let me experience what true love is. Maybe because I had lost a son so many years ago, this is my chance at experiencing what it is to love a child as if he were my own; perhaps this is my chance to know what it would have been like to see my son grow up and become a man. Whatever His reason, I am thankful for the years I have had with you. The road has been bumpy at times with lots of boulders to be removed from our paths; but, low and behold, the Man that can move mountains gently pushed those boulders out of our way and let us move on with our journey in life. I have no regrets for my choice to marry your dad and to have you as a son. We were meant to be mother and son just as Tom and I were meant to be dad and daughter. I hope, even if small, that you take something good from the relationship and experiences you and I have shared.

Gunnar, I have a wonderful relationship with God; but it took me many years to get here and, proudly, I can call myself a Christian. The Lord was always there, but I was stubborn and refused to think that He was the way. I made wrong choices in life even as an adult only to be smacked on my head by the Man upstairs and, fortunately, given another chance to get it right. FINALLY, I learned to stop doing the same thing over and over with my life, stop making choices that I think are fit for me, and stop thinking that I was the one in charge. I realized it took more than just believing in God and praying about things to make me a Christian. You must speak to Him with sincerity from the heart; something I am proud to say I do. He is in my heart when I speak of Him or to Him. NOW, I KNOW that He is my Father in Heaven, and that He listens to my every word and knows my every thought. He is with me EVERY day that I am allowed to live on this earth and, with His forgiveness, He will be with me in my eternal life as well. I love Him so deeply that I can feel within me the grace He grants me. There is happiness in my soul because I have been led by the Light and not the darkness of Satan. One of my prayers for you is that you discover this amazing feeling from deep within yourself and that you find it much sooner in life than I did. If ever I had a regret, it would be that I did not come to know the Lord at a younger age, as I know Him now.

You will be in my prayers this week, Gunnar, as you take the first steps as a young man towards a relationship with God. It will be your own; but, like many others, you also will experience some boulders in the road. Remember, my sweet son, He will remove them if you always put your trust in Him and not man. If ever you feel lost, reach out and take His hand and let the Light guide you. I pray that you always have enough faith to know that He never leaves your side, during good times and bad. There is a life lesson every day we live. Seek Him daily and you will learn the lesson; be faithful to yourself and to your beliefs, but always listen with your heart to what God is trying to teach you. You are a child of God, honey, so honor Him as you should. Trust Him; worship Him; and, above all, follow Him. He is the way, He is the light; and He loves you unconditionally.

With love,

    Brenda

Compliments of God

I met Susie and Kathy about 35 years ago. From the very beginning I was so envious of the relationship they had as sisters and best friends. I am sure they had their ups and downs, especially as kids growing up in the same house. But as adults, what I saw was them sharing the love they had for their mother; the family bond they taught their kids; the fun and laughter; and sadness and sorrows. But through it all, they definitely shared a closeness that I could only dream of.

Dear Lord,

Today I attended a memorial for my friend's sister who was taken from her family and friends much too soon. Lord, thank You for allowing me to experience the kind hearts of so many and for allowing me to be a part of this celebration of life for Kathy. She was so well remembered, so loved and, obviously, one of a kind. Bless her children, her sister Susie, her nieces and nephew, and her many friends with their memories of her. May the stories continue to be shared over the years so her grandchildren will know her, too; and just as Kathy would have wanted, may this celebration of life continue long after today. Rest in peace my friend. In Jesus name. Amen.

Kathy and Susie, sisters and best friends

Julo Spencer

Dear God,

There is always so much to pray for, and at times I am overwhelmed with the needs of others; I just don't know where to start sometimes. But today is not one of those days. Today I want to thank You for watching over the kids and church leaders that are at camp this week. A special thank You for watching over my nephew, Grayson, and allowing him to share this wonderful experience with the other kids. He has grown as a Christian child, and with that, I pray that he continues to build his relationship with You for the rest of his life. May he be the leader of many and invite them to know You as well. My prayer is that You will always remain in his heart, always leading him to do good, to think clearly about right from wrong, and to always strive to please You, our Savior. Thank You for hearing my words. With loving thoughts of Your Son, Jesus. Amen.

Compliments of God

Apology Accepted

As I was standing in line at the grocery store one evening there were a few people in front of me; and, as usual, I was in a hurry and only interested in paying and getting out of there. I stood there looking at the magazine covers as my mind wandered into a world of celebrity. I was jolted out of my daydream when a woman bumped my arm as she reached around me to hand the man in front of me an item she had forgotten. When the man turned to take it from her, I saw that he was my dad. I hesitated to speak to him. I was 23 years old, and we had not seen each other since I was 15. My heart started to pound faster as I tried to muster the courage to say something to him. With mixed emotions, I softly said "Daddy"? His head turned in my direction, and I could see there was puzzlement on his face. Seven years had gone by, and I had grown from a child to a woman. I knew immediately that he didn't even know who I was. I said "Daddy, it's me, your daughter". I saw a bit of a spark of delight as he responded with "oh, I didn't even recognize you". The spark faded quickly as he fidgeted to pay the cashier. It slips my mind as to what the small talk was about, but it was brief, and before I knew it he was gone. Seven years, and neither of us could think of anything to say to each other. There were no hugs or happy-to-see-you smiles. We were just a couple of slightly familiar faces that had run into each other at a local grocery store. I was baffled and a little shaken from seeing him again and the lack of response that we had to each other. As I walked to my car, I shook the feelings off and accepted that our life as father and daughter was never going to be, again.

Just as I reached for the handle on the car door, I heard a voice call out my childhood nickname. A sense of happiness rushed through me as I turned to see my dad standing there. I looked up at him probably with the same expression of admiration on my face that I did when I was a little girl. Daddy reached out, hugged me, then looked me right in the eyes and said "I'm sorry for the times I hit you". With sadness and, I believe maybe a tear in his eye, he asked "will you forgive me?" I bounced my head up and down rapidly numerous times to answer him, then buried my face in his chest as we hugged tightly. For that moment, I felt like I was his little girl again.

My heart had hardened over the years, and the feeling of determination to not get hurt again made me pull away from him. I could feel the strength in his hands and arms release me with reluctance. I think back now and realize the look on his face was of uncertainty in not knowing if I had really forgiven him. I turned to get in my car, cleared my throat, raised my head high, and sat straight and tall in the seat as if to reaffirm that I was okay and that I would not allow him to hurt me again. I drove away without looking back.

I saw daddy only a few times over the years, and the relationship I wanted to have with him never rekindled....until the day of my mother's funeral. I was shocked and in awe to see my dad at mom's service. They had not spoken to each other for at least forty years, and when mom spoke of him it was always vile words of hatred. I approached daddy after the service and thanked him for coming. He explained, "She was the mother of my kids; it was the right thing to do". I can guarantee, had it been the other way around, my mother would not have attended my dad's service.

It was just a month later that my step-mother passed away from complications of a stroke she had a couple of years before. I was never close to her and by the time of her death, it had probably been 20 years since I had seen her. Our time together had been strained to say the least, but in all fairness to her, I was not her daughter and I am sure she had no intentions of taking on three more children when she married daddy. My brother that lived with her the longest, told me that he did not get along with her either but that before she died, she did pull him aside and told him that she was sorry for all the disagreements they had been through; taking most of the blame herself. Her apology to my brother was enough for me to understand what it must have been like for her to add three more kids to her already four and try to love them. Maybe there just wasn't enough love to go around. At any rate, she was my dad's wife and out of respect for him, I went to her service. He had proved to me, by coming to pay his respects to mom, that he was not the bad person I thought he was. I wanted to prove to him that I, too, was not a bad person.

It was early fall, and the weather was beginning to cool. The days of my mother's and step-mother's services had passed, and the families were beginning to return to some normalcy. My brothers and I had been reunited after many years of being torn apart from the long-lasting bitterness of our parent's divorce. We talked and laughed with each other as if the time without each other had never happened. We discovered truths in the reasons for our separation and, with understanding, accepted one another for whom we had become without the influence of the other in our lives. I liked the feeling of having them near me. I was getting to know my siblings and their families; and now it was my chance to get to know daddy, too. With encouragement from one of my brothers, I spent more time with dad. We all tried to get together as often as possible so we could continue the bonding process and not drift apart again.

Autumn was in full bloom by now and Thanksgiving Day was just around the corner. The extended families were almost impossible for us to keep up with; so I decided to do an early Thanksgiving dinner with just my brothers, my sister in-laws, and our dad. They were to do their individual dinners with their kids and grandkids on the traditional Thursday in November.

We all gathered in the living room of my home after we had all enjoyed the fine (if I must say so myself) dinner I had prepared for everyone. My brothers were doing their usual bantering about who-knows-what as their wives made attempts at calming the men down a bit.

Daddy was sitting alone just taking in all the commotion his boys were making with each other. I could see the look of happiness in his face with having his kids together; I also saw some sadness in his eyes. I sat down next to him, patted him lightly, and asked if he was feeling okay. He made the same eye contact with me he had so many years before in the parking of the grocery store; and, once again, apologized for what he had done. My heart sunk to my stomach with the reality of how this had haunted him for so many years. I reassured him that his apology had been accepted many years before, and that I loved him more than life itself.

Our daddy went to be with our Lord in heaven just two days after that Thanksgiving Day in 1999. I cried for days on end with sorrow after he was gone. We had missed so much in our lives with the void of each other, and I was struggling terribly with the stubbornness we both had displayed over the years. It is only now that I find understanding in our last days together and once again I thank God for having His hand in my life. Had the losses over the past few months occurred in any other order, I would never had been reunited with my brothers nor found understanding of my step-mother; And I would have never been able to be daddy's little girl again. God is good.

Daddy, July 23, 1926 to November 27, 1999

Julo Spencer

Dear Lord,

Thank You ever so much for the grandparents of this world, for they are the connection to the roots of our heritage. May we listen as they browse through the pages of time and share the stories of generations past; pulling in their wisdom to share in the future. When we look into the faces of our grandparents may we acknowledge Your gracious love in their eyes. I pray we are always gentle with the elderly and recognize the weaknesses of old age. Please remind us to remain committed to them, even in hardships or times of misunderstanding their words or behavior. May we always honor our grandmothers and grandfathers with respect and love and forever cherish the memories. In Christ Jesus. Amen.

Dear God,

It is a special sight to see a father and son together. There is no relationship quite like the one of a boy and his dad. They impact each other's life with the critical roles they both play; helping each other become the best that they can be. I pray that all fathers and sons connect with each other and listen to one another from their minds and their hearts. Fathers, give advice when asked but always set the example. Sons, ask for advice and remember dad is on the same journey as you. He's just a little further down the road. Share the laughter and never hide the tears. Hug each other tight, and say I love you often. Above all, pray together. A father once wrote, "he was blessed beyond measure". I pray his son echoes the same sentiment. You are both sons of God. Follow Him and rest assured that you will never be without each other. In the name of Jesus. Amen.

For Zack and Josh

All Dogs Go To Heaven

My sweet little dog, Riley died suddenly about four years ago. As sad as I was to lose my dear devoted friend, I do believe this was God's way of taking care of him. He had been sick all of his life; born with Epilepsy and a heart murmur; something the doctors always said would be his doom. He took unwanted meds all of his life to help with the seizures he had far too often. It broke my heart to see his state of confusion as he gradually slipped into the fits of shaking and salivating. I would hold him gently, even sing softly to him, in hopes of calming him down and bringing him back to me in his normal state. Some of these episodes would last longer than others, making me wonder if it was the one that would take him from me. As he aged, the seizures became fewer and farther between; and fortunately he was taken off of the meds he tried so desperately not to take. I could never hide them in any amount of cheese to fool him. He obediently ate the cheese or snack though, because he knew I wanted him to. The days of play time never got old for him. Even in his later years, he loved to run down the hall to fetch the ball. The play time just was a bit shorter than it was when he was a young pup and the breathing much heavier as his poor little heart was working hard to let him enjoy his time. I could tell the murmur was in the advanced stages. The admiration after his evening meal; his happiness of me always returning home and the love on his face as he sat in my lap at the end of the day will linger in my mind always. One cold day in January, he jumped up on the bed to lay next to me in the early hours of the morning; something I rarely let him do. But that morning I thought to myself, his days are short and I want to love him and I want him to know he was loved as much as possible before our time together is gone. We snuggled. I took him with me everywhere I went that day; even allowing him to sit in my lap as I drove; we drove through the car wash together and he did his usual barking as the rainbow colored soaps ran over the windshield, followed by the roar of the rinse. Normally I would hold him to keep him calm so I would not hear the loud bark bounce off the glass of the windows. This day, I let him go as he protectively scared off the big bad machine that was washing our car. He spent the day in my lap as I worked from home that afternoon. The sound of the doorbell interrupted our time together; and, as I opened the door to see who was there, the dog from across the street came out. Riley, ran out the door to greet him but much to his dismay, the truck traveling down the street was not able to stop in time to keep from hitting him. As I think back about the events that day I can't help but think Riley's parting was God's plan. I had prayed not too many days before that God would not let him suffer when his time came. He didn't. It is my belief because there were no physical signs of him being struck, that the sound of the screeching tires that he came face to face with that day, made his heart fail. I was heartbroken; mad at myself for not paying more attention when I opened the door and not being quick minded enough to react and stop him from running out into the street. My comfort is in knowing that is was God's way of answering my prayer, to not let him suffer. It was Riley's time to cross over The Rainbow Bridge. I felt the void in my life; I had times of denial of him being gone; sometimes imagining that he was laying in his favorite spot or thinking I heard him come through his little door from outside. I missed him terribly and I was enlightened to just how much time I spent alone. I decided to find another dog. You see I think Riley was born to be my dog. He was a special needs pet, and God knew I would make sure he was well cared for. He was my baby, God's creation and gift to me. I loved him like he was child.

Now I believe, Jovi, the needy little rescue, was also born to be mine.

I will never forget the day I went to pick him up from one of the animal rescue facilities in town. It was as if the second I stepped through the door, he knew I was his new momma. We made immediate eye contact, his tail wagging and his body wiggling, I walked directly to his crate and took him out. Less than an hour later, we were on our way home together. No doubt, it was God's plan and here today, he lays on my lap as I write the words I share.

Riley- 1999-2011

Jovi- born to us 2011

Genesis 9:16 "Whenever the rainbow appears in the clouds, I will see it and remember the everlasting covenant between God and all living creatures of every kind on the earth."

Lord,

    Thank You so much for creating such a variety of living creatures, especially the ones we call our pets. May we watch over them as one of Your precious creations; never mistreating, underfeeding or overworking them. They are our loyal friends, beloved companions, and part of the family. They fill our hearts with joy and laughter; and, our time with unconditional love. I pray everyone shows compassion towards any and all creatures. May each of us take the time to give or help find a home for the lost or deserted. These sweet, loving animals are a gift from You. May we treasure them as You treasure us. In the name of our Savior, Jesus Christ. Amen.

To Love a Child

Parents: View a step-parent not as a threat or a replacement of you but as an addition to your child's family. Remember the relationship a child has with a step-parent is not about your own insecurities. Be thankful that someone, by their own choice, has chosen to love and teach your child as their own.

Step-parents: You have not conceived or given birth to this child; regardless of the love you feel, you must understand that there is no greater love than that of a mother's or father's. Respect it.

Loving your child is not a competition of which parent loves him or her the most. Everyone is on equal playing ground. Encourage and respect the rules of each household; and give the child the security of knowing each house is, in fact, their "home". With the teachings of God as the center, harmony can be reached. This is something I have prayed about often.

Proverbs 18:21- "Death and life are in the power of the tongue, and those who love it will eat its fruit"

Dear Lord,

The tongue is one of the most powerful tools you have given us. Especially when it comes to raising a child. From the time a child is old enough to understand a person's words, we must begin to speak positive truths into their lives. The deep insight of this truth is seen in all of life. By using kind words, we will breed children that will grow to have warm relationships. If we use harsh words, they will learn only tension and separation. When we speak the truth, we gain trust and confidence; lies break trust and create doubt and suspicion. God, as Your children, You have taught us well; let us use the same rule of thumb as we give our child direction. We must understand that the words we use will affect them as adults in business, friendships, marriage, and faith. May we choose them wisely for they are the center of our relationship with, not only our children, but the world. May the words that roll off the tongues of Your children be Your words; and, Lord, I pray, that the people I meet on this journey share those words with me. In the name of Jesus. Amen.

Brothers

Heavenly Father,

Lord, thank You for these three men You have chosen to be my family. They are so very close to my heart and I want only the best for them. Please renew their minds, bodies and souls as they continue their journey in life. Direct them daily with their decisions in work, family and faith. I pray that they know it is never too late to come to know You. May they use the light You shine so brightly to find their way; asking for forgiveness and surrendering their lives to You. As always, I pray for their families, their good health and their well-being and that we forever remain close. Mostly, God, I pray they know just exactly how much You and I love them. In the name of our Father's Son, Jesus, I thank You once again for the blessing of having them as my brothers. Amen.

Youngest and oldest

Middle

Julo Spencer

Stories to Inspire And Prayers to Comfort

Dear Lord,

    Thank You for the beginning of yet another month of this year. You have led many of us through challenges but also given us many reasons to be joyful and celebrate life. May today, the first day of the new month, be a time of commitment to forgive others and to seek forgiveness, to love and to share our knowledge of You. May love flourish wherever it is missing. I pray that we set our intentions to make this month a time to repent of our sins and grow in Your image. In the name of the Son of God, Jesus, Amen.

God's Design

Our senses are to hear, see, feel, smell, and taste...all of which we sometimes take for granted. Every morning you wake up, take the time to thank God for being able to see the blue sky or the sweet smile on your child's face; thank Him for the sound of the perking water in the coffee pot and the smell of it as it begins to brew. Enjoy and be thankful for the sweet flavor of the breakfast strudel that your colleague shares with you at work. Return the touch of a gentle hand from a loved one, or maybe give an extra pat to the dog or cat that has brushed against you this morning. These are the simple pleasures that without our eyes, nose, ears, tongue, and hands we could not experience. If you have all or any, be thankful, that we have a God that is good.

GREENER PASTURES

Have you ever been told that "the grass is not greener on the other side"? I beg to differ with that statement.

Pay attention to how the rains that God provides makes the grass and plants so green; the flowers perk up and the color of the blossoms are much brighter. When the clouds have cleared, you see the little critters emerge from their shelter and the birds begin to sing again. The long faces of the children that have been cooped up inside until the rain passes turn their frowns upside down and into smiles. Suddenly you hear the sound of them giggling as they run through the back yard or perhaps from a school yard in the distance. The sun breaks through and shines on all of creation. All these things are not of man. These acts of nature is the Light of God performing some of the things He does best.

So many times in my life I have done things against my better judgment. To deliberately sin against God is, no doubt, the dark side of someone's life. I thought that if I did something "wrong" and it didn't really hurt anyone, what's the big deal? And the really ignorant part is I thought I was getting away with it. One day a light went off in my little pea-sized brain. I realized I was, in fact, hurting someone. I was hurting Him. And, for sure, I was not getting away with anything. I vowed right then and there to forget about the darkness of man; to forget about any thoughts of what man expected of me and any thoughts of man's opinion and/or judgment of me. I turned my life, wholeheartedly, over to God. I made a plan to follow Jesus.

The darkness of my sinful life soon started to brighten from within. It wasn't the events in my life so much, and certainly not the things I had acquired, that made the difference. It was the hand of God and my relationship with Him that was bringing the light in. Just as the flowers that bloom from the sun and rain, my life began to flourish. I found peace with all the little things; the rain, a smile, the giggle of a child, or the wag of my dog's tail. The life I had chosen with my husband took on new meaning and purpose for me. I found understanding and forgiveness of those that I thought had wronged me; I found love for all God's children; no matter the color of their skin, or what sins they might have committed.

Often in my life I have asked myself "why" is this happening to me, or "how" could so-and-so do this to me? As I grow older, I gain knowledge and experience and more moments of revelation and insight on life. I figured out it was not someone else that made me create those two questions. It was myself. For me, the "why" was "WHY had I taken so long to come to know the way of Jesus?" And the "how" was "HOW could I have ever hurt Him the way I did?" I kept saying to myself "if only".

Dear Lord,

I pray that all of your children learn to leave the darkness of man behind. May their eyes be opened to the "why" and "how" of their life; and may they, too, decide to follow Jesus. I pray they grow in faith and find satisfaction and complete happiness with the simple things of Your Creation. May they always allow the Light to shine brightly as they discover inner peace in knowing that "the grass IS, most definitely, greener on the other side." In the name of our Savior, Jesus Christ. Amen.

Dear God,

In all of Your creation, I am not sure there is anything more beautiful than the sun rising up at the dawn of day, stretching its arms of light upward and outward as if to say "Good morning. Come enjoy this God-given day with me". Lord, thank You for the Light that allows us to stretch our arms upward and outward, to welcome our family and friends; and, above all, You into our life. May we spread our cheer to others so they too may rise each day with faith and happiness. I pray that our first thoughts bring a smile to our face; and our first words to You, spoken out loud, are of thankfulness for yet another day You have provided. I pray in Jesus' name. Amen.

It Could Be Worse

I, like others, have suffered through trials in my life. I am not proud of the fact that I have two failed marriages and one annulment under my belt. I am not fond of bringing up my childhood and the mother that did not like me. I spent years apart from my dad and my siblings. I was physically abused as a child and adult; and I have been destitute, just short of the point of selling myself to survive.

At a young age I suffered the loss of two children; one to an auto accident while still an infant and the other at birth. I had three miscarriages by the time I was 35. It goes without saying that it was not in the cards for me to have children of my own. I have used the loss of my children as a measure of just exactly what a person can endure in life. Although never a totally clear day, I figure if I can weather that specific storm of life, I can make it through anything.

As I reflect back on my trials, I realize that there is truth in the phrase "something good can come from something bad". The lessons I learned about life from various events and some of the choices I made is, partly, the key to who I am today. I'd like to share just a few of those.

Number one lesson: God is always with me, even though I didn't think so for many years. The heartache and the trials are part of the lessons I was to be taught. With time, they have come to make sense to me. It is not for me to ask why God took my children but for me to accept His plan. I'd like to think that He was just making heaven a little more perfect. I was able to still experience motherhood through my step-children. Jeffrey, now a grown man, was my number one blessing, and I love him to this day. He accepted me with kindness and love and allowed me to love him. I hope he knows just how much.

I also had two step-daughters for a short time. We were never close but it was an experience within itself, and one I don't wish to ever repeat. I will choose having boys over girls, any day. I now have a fourth step-child, and happily he is a boy.

Another lesson is just because a person says he or she believes in God does not make him or her a Christian. For years I dressed up and went to church as if to fool and/or impress others. I associated with men and women that claimed to be God fearing and God loving souls. They could lay hands of comfort on you in troubled times, quote the perfect Bible verse to fit a person's needs, and even express sadness or understanding on their face. But they were just words; their actions proved to be otherwise that of a Christian. Minutes after comforting someone, words of judgment left their lips; they spent their nights drinking, carousing, lying and cheating, and in the morning they would rise and begin their day once again with a facade of portraying a Christian. It opened my eyes to the definition of "talk the talk". Very much ashamed, I disassociated myself with the phonies that surrounded me and gave up the way of life **they** thought I should lead. With pleasure, I closed that chapter of my life and opened a new one by "walking the walk".

Because I grew up very poor, I spent a good part of my adult life seeking and worshiping the all mighty dollar. With that said, the third, but not final lesson I have learned is, money cannot and does not buy happiness. In fact, it can bring some rather large heartaches should you decide to let it consume you. There was a time in my life that I did. The person I wanted everyone to believe was happy and had it all became the person that didn't care what anyone thought. The things I had, became nothing more than just "things". The homes, cars, private jets, social activities, and oh my gosh, all the clothes, were left behind. I walked away from that lifestyle and, with no regret, left nothing but fingerprints of the person I once was. These days, no amount of money will ever impress me nor buy me away from the riches that abound me with the life I have been blessed with today.

The best lesson, although I know not the last I am to learn in life, is love. It is not an "on-the-surface" emotion. For years I honestly did not know what it meant to love someone from the heart. I chose my mates based more on a lifestyle I could live and my friends were chosen with a strategy of who could add something to my life. Thankfully, because of the people God has placed in my life, I have finally learned to feel and express my feelings of true love, from my heart.

I feel joyful love by being reunited with my brothers. I feel maternal love for the children that have been a part of my life. My connection with my friends is a strong love that without words, is often expressed. I share the love of my extended family with others, always staying in touch, showing concern and forever praying for their well-being.

My husband, the man I now consider my purpose for living, is the one man I can say I chose for all the right reasons. He is true to his beliefs and faithful to God; he is intelligent, a hard worker, full of dry wit but often very funny. He is especially a devoted father, son, brother and husband. He loves me unconditionally and he is the one man I can finally trust with my heart. I love him dearly. I know, without a doubt, that it was God's hand that brought us together.

So, I hope from what I have shared, you will come to know just exactly where your journey of trials and tribulations might lead you. You must believe there is a lesson to be learned from all of life's events; good and bad. If you find yourself in a state of sadness or the feeling of being dealt a raw deal because of something "bad" that has happened in your life, try to dig deep within yourself, down to your soul, and pull out "that something good". It's there if you look hard enough. Your life will be more at peace when you find it; and any anger, bitterness, lack of trust, unhappiness, or loneliness will be washed away. Once you discover "the good", take the time to look up, smile, and thank God for teaching you the lesson behind it. Remember it could be worse.

Dear Lord,

Thank you for being in control of my life when I thought I was. Had You let me take the wheel, only You know where I might have ended up. With You by my side, I know the bumps in the road were only pebbles compared to the mountains of blessings You have bestowed upon me. Lord, let me never forget that regardless of what bad experiences I may encounter, there is always someone else that is going through something worse. May I always reach out and show compassion for those in need. Thank You God for loving me so much and for teaching me to love You from deep within my heart. In Christ name, I pray. Amen.

Dear God,

    I know there are many sad and lonely people in the world. The loneliness is sometimes overwhelming and to some, embarrassing. So much so, that it is covered up with a facade of humor or lightheartedness, when in reality, they are hurting and only crying out on the inside. Lord, I pray for all of these lost souls with the faith that they will turn to You in times of despair. May we all pray for one another, and continue to study the Word, because like the Lone Cypress, on the Rock, we will grow in self-worth by the Light and You will give us strength to sustain the darkest of storms. It is in Your Son's name, Jesus, I pray. Amen.

THINGS

When we are children it's all about who has the coolest toy; as teenagers we are into the designer jeans, purses, or whatever the fad may be; and when we become adults it's our job title, house, car; and, even still, our designer jeans.

Hello God,

Please forgive me for all that I think I deserve. For so many years, I thought it was me that was taking care of my needs; only to learn, far too late in life, that it was You all along. For whatever the reasons, You have chosen to bless me with all of life's desires, and I thank You from my heart. Please never let me think that what I have, where I have been, or what I do defines me.

Today I pray that each one of Your children not let 'material things' control their lives. May we all release them so that Your perfect will is done. Let us come to know the true following of Christ is in our heart and what we do for or give, to others. A well-paying job only makes us successful in the eyes of our peers. The new Mercedes or Harley only gets us from point A to point B. It does not get us to the gates of Heaven. The designer clothes may make us feel prettier or more handsome, but the true beauty comes from within. God, You are our success; You are the grand Designer, and it is You that will lead us to the gates of Heaven. Please do not let me be the person that spews words that shine only on me. May I never hoard in fear of "being without", but trust that You will always provide my needs. From this day forward may each day be a day of "giving" to someone more deserving. With a thankful heart I pray in the name of Jesus. Amen.

"But understand this: If the owner of the house had known at what hour the thief was coming, he would not have let his house be broken into." Luke 12:39

Dear Lord,

  Our normal day-to-day tasks are generally "routine", and we tend to look to You to help guide us through our daily activities. If we get out of the routine of the workplace or our daily chores, we are often caught off guard by the enemy of our souls. Idle time is a place in our lives that Satan seeks us with hopes of drawing us away from You. God, please always remind us that we must continue our spiritual routine even during leisurely times like vacation or a day off from work or school. May we avoid the test of our character as we carry on with our daily prayers; always giving thanks for our many blessings and miracles You have bestowed upon us. Remind us to be on guard from Satan and to use our times of retreat for spiritual refreshment and not just physical refreshment. If we do this, our faith tells us that You will keep the thief from entering our house. Thank You Lord for hearing our prayers. In Jesus' name, Amen

Dear Lord,

More often than not, when we comfort someone that has lost a loved one, we say they have gone to live in a better place. Lord, I believe that to be the understatement of my lifetime. It is blissful, full of peace, and happiness, and LOVE. And the best part, we get to see You face to face. I pray today that everyone I know that has lost someone important in their life holds on to their memory until they see them again in Heaven. May we find peace in believing that those that have gone before us are watching us, smiling down at us, and saying do not worry about me. I AM in a better place; and soon we will be side by side again, laughing and sharing the Kingdom of God together. It is Your promise to us if we live the life on earth You have instructed. Let us give to others, love without judgment, forget about vanity and self, and do only the good You want us to do; believing that if we repent out loud and from our heart You will reward us with eternal life, and the loved ones we miss so dearly will be waiting for us at one of the Gates of Heaven.

Thank You Lord for all You do and give to us daily. If we are not deserving of those blessings, may we look deep within our soul and change our ways TODAY so that You will be happy with us and let us live out the Promise. With a humble heart, I pray in the name of Jesus. Amen

Dear God,

    Thank You for this new day of opportunity full of amazing things You offer each of us. Let us face today with no regrets of the past, but only lessons learned. May we count our blessings and go forth with what You have provided, using the tools You have granted us to speak and practice the Word. I thank You for the people you have placed in my life that are here TODAY. I thank You for what my eyes can see and my ears can hear TODAY. I thank You for the love You have placed in my heart TODAY. May we have FAITH in our future and know that only You will allow our love to overflow into tomorrow and bring us yet another new "TODAY", full of opportunity and amazing Goodness. Thank You, Lord, for the peace I have in knowing You. You are my Light, You are the Way, and, because You have taught me so well, I know You are my "TODAY". In Christ, I pray. Amen.

The past was yesterday, the future is tomorrow, but today is our Present....let us live it as such.

Dear Lord,

Thank you so very much for blessing the area I live in with the falling water. I pray that all the drought ridden areas are so blessed with rain. Please fill the lakes and rivers; please water the crops and orchards; please give drink to the animals of the wild and their land so they may survive. Glory to You for all that You provide, Lord. In Jesus' name. Amen

Luke 23:42-Then he said, "Jesus, remember me when you come into your kingdom." 43 Jesus answered him, "Truly I tell you, today you will be with me in paradise." (Jesus speaking to the thief on the cross.)

Many years ago, while going through a divorce, someone broke into my apartment. Though nothing of any monetary value was taken, a very large box, full of a lifetime of photos, was. You can't put a price on something like that. I thought it was one of the meanest things a person could do to another, especially if the thief knew my past and how important the items in the box were to me. There would never be another opportunity to get a picture of my son or parents. My childhood, pictures of my siblings, the kids I went to high school with and the pages of photos of gatherings and events with family; all gone.

Dear God,

    I feel anger from within when I, or someone I love, is wronged by another. Your will is for me to pray for such a villain rather than maliciously seek revenge. That is difficult sometimes, but I know the power of prayer is strong. Please lead me to pray for them. May their hearts be softened; may they honor You by not rejoicing in another's pain or loss; may they send well wishes for another's accomplishments rather than trying to set them up for failure. Please let the meanness that lurks within them be cast out by Your love and grace. And, Lord, please keep MY heart soft towards others' feelings and needs. May I always be the child of God that finds pleasure in doing the right thing, bringing joy to myself and pleasure to You. Thank You for hearing my prayers. Lovingly, I pray in the name of Jesus. Amen.

I support Pro-Life. Scripture clearly calls us to protect and defend the innocent and that, most certainly, includes the unborn. I believe that abortion is an attack on the Church and the Body of Christ.

Job 31:15 -Did not God make him as well as me? Did he not give us life in our mothers' bodies?

Dear God,

I thank You for the gift of my life and for all the lives of my family and friends. Today I commit myself to never be silent about abortion and to never forget the unborn. I pray for all the innocent little souls that die in the womb of their mother and that You will give them eternal life. Lord, please extend Your hand of protection and help put an end to the evil of abortion. May each woman's eyes be open to this gift of life they carry and know that to end it is going against all You have taught us. I pray that adoption be an alternative. It can be an answer to a prayer for many couples that cannot conceive their own offspring and, certainly, a favorable alternative for the child. May Your spirit live deep within us so that we will always know that life is good and that no unborn child is dismissed as less valuable than those who are born. In the name of Jesus Christ, the Son of God. Amen.

1 Corinthians 3:16-17 -Do you not know that you are God's temple and that God's Spirit dwells in you? If anyone destroys God's temple, God will destroy him. For God's temple is holy, and you are that temple.

God's Timing

Yesterday as I worked on a two-week project of tearing out and replanting a large flower bed the skies became cloudy, the winds picked up, and the temperatures dropped. Thinking that I would never get all the work done before the rains hopefully came; I stopped and put all my tools away. I needed one more thing to complete the job. Off to the nursery my husband and I go to get some mulch so I can add the finishing touches and be done. While out and about the sun returned, it was somewhat warm again and the wind had died down a bit. Home again and mulch unloaded, I stared at it thinking that it was not enough; so I decided to put those grubby clothes back on and put the mulch down so I could see how much more I might need to pick up on Monday morning and complete the job another day. About half way through the process the clouds rolled in and the cool winds picked up again. I seriously stood up to face the wind and thanked God for cooling me off. Well, lo and behold, ten bags later (the perfect amount) I was able to clean up and stand back and admire my work. Should I water or not…hmm. I'll wait. Fresh clothes, my coffee in hand; and, of course Jovi by my side, I sat on the back porch to rest. Literally just minutes later, praise God, rain started falling from the sky; watering all the newly planted shrubs and flowers. It was a beautiful sight and it was all God's perfect timing.

Dear Lord,

I know we all want good things to happen in our lives and, of course, we want them "now". I pray that we all learn to put our trust in You and Your plan. We spend so much of our lives worrying and being impatient that only leads to frustration and disappointment. Our plans are not always the best for us. Yours are. You are never late but often You are not early either. You let us wait to stretch our faith in You. In trusting You, having faith that Your plan is the best for us, we accept change and grow. May we pray about the things we want and need; and believe that no matter how small or large our prayer to You is, it will be granted and questions will be answered if we wait. I ask that You grant us patience with the changes in our lives; with all situations we think we need the answers to NOW, and that we learn from the difficult as well as the good times. You give us hopes and dreams for certain things to happen in our lives; and, so often, we want to give up because it is "taking too long". But just like the rain yesterday, we must accept Your timing. May we all learn to live with hope and enjoy life, knowing that You are working on our problems and entrust ourselves to You so we can experience total peace and happiness. Thank You, Lord, for the rain; thank You for Your plan. In the name of Jesus and my love for You, my Savior I pray. Amen.

I Saw God Today

Where did you see Him? Was it in your backyard when a pair of ducks visit in the spring; was it the calmness of trees swaying in the breeze as you have your morning coffee; was it on your child's face as he or she rubbed the their eyes to wake from their slumber; was it the soft touch of your husband or wife that without words says "good morning"; was it in the sunrise, the blue sky, or the white clouds? Wherever you are, whatever you look at today, I pray that you see God.

Dear God,

There is no condition that is too difficult for You. By Your hand You have given man the ability to create medicines and techniques that help heal the sick, and I am thankful for that. But we must never neglect prayer and the power it has over healing. It is a treatment path that is free, available to all, and has no negative side effects. God, Your power is enormous. So today I pray that everyone be open for opportunity, and pray every chance they get. When someone asks us to pray for them or a loved one, may we stop what we are doing and pray. Let us pray with true sincerity and never stop with just one prayer. As Your children we must never give up. We need each other in times of distress, illness, or loss. May we all be the person YOU want us to be and the person WE want to be and project to others. May we be there for one another to lend a helping hand, to talk or just listen; and, above all truly with heart, pray for one another. Today, in the name of Jesus', I pray for my friend who has cancer. For her sister, her children, and her friends that will walk the path of a fearful journey with her. Please, Lord, I ask that You be with them always. And may they be forever faithful, always praying, and never giving up on the Power of Your healing. Thank You, Lord, for the Promise of eternal life. May all glory be to You, our Savior. In Your Son's name, Jesus. Amen.

More than the sounds of many waters, than the mighty breakers of the sea, The LORD on high is mighty. –

Dear Lord,

Once, again, I am amazed at the beauty of Your Creation. I feel so much at peace while walking on the beach and hearing the sound of the ocean waves brushing up against the sandy shores, washing up seashells for our choosing; the cawing of the gulls and pelicans as they fly overhead and dip down into the sea for their morning meal; the giant turtle tracks in the sand that were left during the darkness of the night and early morn; the magnificence of Your artwork in the sky with the colors You choose when the sun rises over the water. Thank You for serving me up with this chicken soup for the soul. And, Lord, thank You for my husband, Duncan, who never deprives me of this trip with my friend every year. I am blessed. In the loving name of Your Son, Jesus, Amen.

Heavenly Father,

I ask today that anyone facing stress with financial concerns, workplace deadlines, relationships- whatever it is that is creating stress on them, that they turn to You with confidence and that they will find peace. May they take that first step to spiritual authority by not falling prey to the devil's lies; that they find peace within themselves to overcome their circumstances. Peace will overwhelm Satan and shatter any lies or temptations and send demons fleeing. *"Yea, though I walk through the valley of the shadow of death, I will fear no evil; for Thou art with me" – Psalm 23:4a.*

Like David, our trust must lie with You through every battle in life. There is no adversity that will not unfold in victory if we maintain our faith in You. You are the source of peace, and I fear nothing with You at my side. Thank You Father for always being here with us. In the name of the Son of God, Jesus, Amen.

Lord,

You are seated on the Holy throne and reign over all the nations. Your will is done as You speak words of vengeance and protection. You are a mighty fortress. Lord, please protect us and guide us to be united for You. May we live for You and minister to one another, spreading the Word to the rest of the world as you so desire. May You be praised forever. In Jesus' name, Amen.

This is a letter to a friend that had requested some help with a friend of his. Perhaps this is something you are looking for too.

Good afternoon my friend,

I don't know that this is really what your friend is looking for in the form of a prayer, but maybe it will get her started. I can add a lot more if you think I should. Basically, I think what is most wanted and needed by cancer patients is listening, showing compassion and understanding that unless a person is suffering with the same cancer, there is no way to know what they are going through. That's why I added the part about clichés or fix-it responses. I know a woman who is very strong in her faith; she never gave up on prayer and miracles. She was Stage 4 with a very dismal future; miraculously she is here today, cancer free. It was a tough road for her and she is still weak but love, hope, faith, and support of her loved ones gives her more and more strength every day. I would suggest to this lady you speak of, that she ask her friend what it is she wants from everyone. Continued phone messages, texts, emails, cards, prayers, etc., will help brighten her days; but everyone should understand that the days ahead for her are tough ones, and that just because they send her a message does not mean they will hear back from her. She will be tired, weak, depressed and, overall, just not in the mood to respond; but that does not mean others should stop showing support for her. Remember she is the one that is sick….this is about her, not them. I will continue to show my support for her and offer prayer. As you know there are never too many prayers for any one human being. The miracle will be granted if it is God's will. Blessings to you always, Ron, for your continued faith in our Lord and Savior.

Dear Lord,

I come to You today and reach out in prayer because, as You know, one of my friends is not feeling well. Lord, please give her strength and the continued faith to know that with Your hand, anything is possible; that YOU and her friends and family are here if she needs us for anything- anything at all. God, I will do all I can in my power for her. If it is sympathy she needs, I will give it to her; if she is scared, I will remind her that she is human but she can still fight this; if she is weak, I will hold her up; if she wants to talk; I will listen with my heart and offer my gift of prayer, never using clichés or fix-it responses. May comfort and hope be found in hearing success stories…people who beat cancer even in the late stages. I pray that my friend will allow others to walk alongside her down this path of hope to wellness and that she knows she is never alone. May we all keep our word to her and to You by fulfilling the promises to help when needed and to take the time to stay in touch with words of love and continued prayers. God, thank You for Your love and for all You give to us. May none of us ever discount the power of prayer and the many miracles that have happened along this journey we call life. In Jesus' name I pray and ask with love in my heart that You use my friend as a witness to yet another miracle. Amen.

Matthew 17:20 He replied, "Because you have so little faith. I tell you the truth, if you have faith as small as a mustard seed, you can say to this mountain, 'Move from here to there' and it will move. Nothing will be impossible for you."

Good Morning God,

    I know that so many of your children are looking for real faith and many place their faith in the wrong god. It may be a false god or material things or maybe another person. Today I pray that You will use me and my accumulation of life experiences to demonstrate what REAL faith is to all non-believers. I pray there are opportunities to share my faith and that You give me all the right words to say to influence those who need it. Lord, I am Your servant. Please speak through me and work through me. In Jesus' name pray, Amen.

Dear God,

    Father, You parted the Red Sea for Moses and the people of Israel. Their faith gave them the obedience as they stepped out into the moving waters. I face Red Seas in life, too, that sometimes make me feel helpless or not certain of what is ahead of me. Please continue to give me the courage, and let me remain in faith so I may always step out and follow You. Thank You for being with me as I move through my journey of life, forever helping me through difficult decisions and circumstances. I know You are with me, just as You were with Moses as he crossed the Red Sea. Glory to You for all that is done. In Jesus' name, Amen.

Dear Lord,

Today, I want to thank You for the gift of social media. Through modern technology You have connected us with the rest of the world. You have given us the ability to communicate YOU to a generation who needs to see You clearly. You have created a community that can capture an audience of millions who will spread Your words and let You be known to all nations. Lord, I pray that each person reading this, each person using social media will use it in such a way that honors You, our Savior. May we use this gift of technology to uplift others with words of inspiration and encouragement and point them to a relationship with You. Lord, let not Your children that use social media be viewed as losers who have nothing better to do than spend their time on the internet, but let them be seen and heard as Your messengers that testify to His grace and truth. May it not be used for sins of lust and idolatry but for righteousness, faith, love, prayer and all to Your glory. Thank You God for these friends.

Thank You for their shared words, photos, places, and events. Thank You for letting us be there for one another at a time of loss, loneliness or despair. Thank You for all the laughter we share even when sometimes it's at our own expense. Most of all Lord, thank You for this connection that allows us to share You. In the name of the Son of God, Jesus, Amen.

Dear God,

    Lord, may we speak the Word and pray the Word. May each of us reach out believing that there is power in prayer to turn the lost from darkness to light and from the power of Satan to You so forgiveness of sins will be received. I pray today that everyone reading this will share with others so the power of prayer will spread the world over. Please see the palms of "our hands" clasp together in prayer so we will see "Your hands" at work. Satan may influence the fortune tellers of this world to look into the palms of the hands of many, but Jesus paid the price to redeem a lost humanity and His vision for us to become His very own is so far reaching that in the Old Testament He even stated:

Isaiah 49:16 See, I have engraved you on the palms of my hands; your walls are ever before me.

    Every time Your Son opens His nail scarred hands, He is reminded of His unconditional love for Your children. Surely, if "He has the whole world in His hands," then by faith, He has destined souls there also. Thank You for letting us know that because of Your promise, our faith and with prayer we have received salvation, been restored, felt healing, shared miracles, seen signs and wonders and been rescued from moral corruption and evil. Like never before, may we put the palms of "our hands" together in outreach prayer and as we say the words be reminded of what "Jesus did with His"! In the Holy name of Your Son, Jesus. Amen.

Peace I leave with you; my peace I give you. I do not give to you as the world gives. Do not let your hearts be troubled and do not be afraid. -- *John 14:27 (NIV)*

1 John 2:9 Whoever says he is in the light and hates his brother is still in darkness.

Heavenly Father,

It seems bullying has become an epidemic of sorts in society. Children in school feel so inferior to their peers that parents allow them to stay home for fear of their child being hurt physically and more so emotionally thus depriving the child from social activities and an education. Plastic surgery is now being sought by the young just so they will be accepted in a world that was once based on the Christian values You have written for us to obey.

Leviticus 19:18 18 You shall not take vengeance or bear a grudge against the sons of your own people, but you shall love your neighbor as yourself: I am the Lord.

Adults are bullied at work by an overbearing employer or supervisor who treat others as inferiors in order to increase their self-worth. Injustice surfaces during divorce and attempts to defraud one another in order to ruin a reputation for self-gain. Lord, I ask that You please watch over the person that is being bullied, be it child or adult, and let them not be judged by others as being less valuable, less worthy, degraded or ignored. Please take each one of these persons into Your heart and give them strength, peace and justice. And more so, please convert the offenders and give them just humility and respect of others. May they know that when they laugh at someone, that person feels pain; when they pick on someone there is anger but also fear; and when we don't stick up for someone that is being bullied, we let them feel alone. May none of us ever have to say "I'm sorry" again because of something hurtful we have said or done to another. Thank You, Lord, for the reminder of our own fears and loneliness so we may strive to protect someone in need. In the name of Jesus, I pray for all who are bullied and for all who bully. Amen.

Julo Spencer

Good morning Lord,

    Thank you for this day. Thank You for the times when I can step back and reflect and realize just how blessed of a life You have given me. I realize that through the years, I have developed habits that are irritating to You...and to many others. Please help me work on changing those bad habits. And please help me be more patient with my friends and family who may have irritating quirks that can get on my last nerve. I ask that You forgive me of my sins and failures, and all the times I have not been kind to my family, friends and strangers. I offer a commitment to You today, that with Your help, I will change for the better. I praise and worship You, Lord. In Jesus' name. Amen.

Dear God,

Today I am thankful for YOU because without You I would have nothing. May there be many blessings on this Thanksgiving Day to everyone all over the world. Amen.

Dear Lord,

Today is Friday--the day after Thanksgiving Day in the USA. People flock to the malls and outlets to spend more money than any other day of the year. There are sales to catch, gifts to buy, and debts to incur. God, please give us an extra nudge, wisdom, and, the desire to live within our means today and in the days to come. You gave us a very special gift because of Your love for us. We should not give to others out of a sense of duty, but because we love or appreciate them. Help us to remember that the gifts we buy are nowhere near as important as the gift of our time and love. Lord, I want to enjoy the simple pleasures of life and make time for my friends and family this Christmas season. Thank You so much for Your priceless gift of Your Son and the salvation You so lovingly provided for me. In my Savior's name, Jesus, I pray. Amen.

OH, MY WORD!!!

A friend of mine introduced me to a book that was written about using words to change your life. Each year I am to choose a word that can make a difference in my life. I actually have to use it on a regular basis for it to "make the difference". At first the idea sounded hokey to me, but the more I thought about it, I decided maybe it's worth a shot. I bought the book, read it, and took to heart what the guys that wrote it were trying to say. I am a creature of habit, but I have come to know myself well enough to know that an action can become habit very quickly. I pondered on what word would make a difference in my life over the course of a year. Several came to mind but most of them were words that just sounded pretty or pleasant. I needed to think harder….outside the box, so to speak. I was lying in bed one morning, PONDERING on if I should get up or lie in bed for a while longer. Suddenly the word, my word, came to me. Immediately I threw the covers back, turned on the coffee pot, and sat down at the computer to write my word down and what it would do for me during the next twelve months. Here is my word.

MOVE

First things first; I am going to MOVE back into God's house and listen to and learn more from His word.

I hope to MOVE people's hearts with my words that God gives me: be it words of scripture, fact, encouragement, sympathy, empathy, and definitely laughter.

I will MOVE out of the fast lane of life and into the slow lane so I am able to stop quickly, take in what is around me, and enjoy my journey.

I will finally act on my plan to MOVE towards new hobbies and adventures; take an art class or photography class; travel to somewhere I have never been before; read and write more; volunteer.

I fancy a smaller butt so maybe I should MOVE it more…my hand to my mouth less. MOVE over candy, cakes, cookies and ice cream and make room for the fruits and veggies this year. (Do chocolate-covered cherries count as a fruit?) God please give me strength to MOVE right past that baking isle at the grocery store and the candy bins by the check-out counter. This will be a tough MOVE for me.

I love people and want them to love me so my wish is to MOVE them into my heart and myself into theirs. To MOVE with love is the way to build trust and lifelong relationships.

I need to re-MOVE criticism and anger from my tongue and, with my inside-voice, use words of patience and understanding.

I strive to be a better wife, mother, friend, and sister so I will continue to MOVE towards that goal.

Last, but not least, I ask that the person reading this now will believe in me, take my hand, and MOVE with me in the coming year.

Good morning Lord,

I know through experience what it is like to lose someone dear, during the holiday season. Honestly I miss them no more this time of year than I do the rest. Thank You for touching my life with comfort and peace. I ask that you please give the same comfort, peace and strength to others that have lost a loved one. Christmas is so often a time of family gatherings and special memories, in addition to being a time to celebrate the birth of the Savior. We share love and fresh thoughts with those dear to us. It is also a time that leaves some lonely. Lord I pray that the hurting, the grieving, the lonely will feel Your presence in their lives in a real way. I pray that You will fill that place in their hearts with the peace only You can provide. May their memories be sweet and precious jewels in their minds. Let there be friends, family, neighbors, and brothers and sisters in Christ there to encourage and bring cheer to those that are in need of a shoulder or an ear. Thank you for those blessings, loving Father. In the name of Your Son, Jesus. Amen.

Dear Lord,

As Christmas nears, the shopping, tree trimming and parties will soon be behind us. Mankind has commercialized the Christmas season with the various shades of red and green, bright twinkling lights, Santa Claus, parades and parties, and an overwhelming amount of gift giving. Lord I hope You will forgive us if it is wrong to celebrate so lavishly with the manmade traditions; but I do believe deep within the hearts and souls of each Christian man and woman remains the true meaning of Christmas. It is a time to express our love and gratitude to not only You, but to each other. If no other, the Christmas season is the one time we reach out to people in need; we indulge our families and friends with fine meals, homemade gifts and time together; and, for some, it is the ONE day of the year that is set aside for worship.

There are expressions of love and the celebration of Your Son's birth with private time of prayer and even through song. Lord, I hope each of us follow in the footsteps of the Son that You blessed us with on the holy night we call Christmas. Let us listen for the sound of sandaled feet and reach out for the Carpenter's hand. May we discover it is true that He reveals Himself during our conflicts and sufferings and that He is not just the Babe in Bethlehem but the greatest teacher to ever live. I pray that for those who have not, will come to know Him as the Son of God, our Savior and our Redeemer. And may He not only be our focus during this holy season but with every changing season of all the years to come. In the name of the Holy name of Jesus Christ and the Son of God, Amen.

HE IS THE REASON FOR THE SEASON

Dear Lord,

    Please fill every heart with Your peace and the hope You have given us through Your son, our Savior, Jesus Christ. I pray that You will lift the spirits of all Your children and that they will experience Your joy and feel the warmth of Your presence. Father, thank You for the gift of salvation through Jesus and the comfort of the Holy Spirit You sent to guide us. Thank You for the shining light that comes from only Your Word; the true light.

1 In the beginning was the Word, and the Word was with God, and the Word was God. 2 He was with God in the beginning. 3 Through him all things were made; without him nothing was made that has been made. 4 In him was life, and that life was the light of all mankind. 5 The light shines in the darkness, and the darkness has not overcome it.

6 There was a man sent from God whose name was John. 7 He came as a witness to testify concerning that light, so that through him all might believe. 8 He himself was not the light; he came only as a witness to the light.

9 The true light that gives light to everyone was coming into the world. 10 He was in the world, and though the world was made through him, the world did not recognize him. 11 He came to that which was his own, but his own did not receive him. 12 Yet to all who did receive him, to those who believed in his name, he gave the right to become children of God— 13 children born not of natural descent, nor of human decision or a husband's will, but born of God.

14 The Word became flesh and made his dwelling among us. We have seen his glory, the glory of the one and only Son, who came from the Father, full of grace and truth.

    Thank You for who You are and all You do. I love You. Amen

Merry Christmas.

A NEW YEAR

Don't worry about anything, but in all your prayers ask God for what you need, always asking him with a thankful heart. Philippians 4:6 (GNT)

Dear God,

With the passing of the old year, a new one is born. One of the great things about walking with You in life is that with each new dawn there is always the opportunity to start anew, so today I begin my day with thanking You for the days ahead. I know these are Your gifts to us that will carry blessings to all that honor and give glory to You. May each of us leave the bad behind and focus only on the good. May we all have new hope, find peace and experience joy. May we start the New Year with a clean heart and learn to forgive more and hate less. Thank You for this new beginning on earth and for all the potential the future holds. May there be a mighty flame kindled in all of us so that in our time, many will see the wonders of You, our God, and live forever to praise Your glorious name. Amen.

May God bless you all.

Dear God,

Lord, You have given me purpose in life and, through the Bible, I know what You expect of me. Sometimes I am disappointed when I expect a friend, family member, or even a co-worker to do what they say they will do; or to take some responsibility for their actions. It can make me angry or, at times, hurt my feelings. Lord, I know I must disappoint You sometimes too; and, for that, I am sorry. Please forgive me for my shortcomings. Grant me the patience that You have with me so I may have it with others when I feel the frustrations of unmet expectations. I pray that I do not speak out in anger but instead use words of kindness and understanding. I ask for Your forgiveness during these times. In the name of the Son of God, Jesus, Amen.

"For the wages of sin is death; but the gift of God is eternal life through Jesus Christ our Lord" (Romans 6:23).

Dear Lord,

    Thank You for Your gift of eternal life through Your Son, Jesus. Your love and passion is shown in that act of redemption. *"For He made Him who knew no sin to be sin for us, that we might become the righteousness of God in Him" (2 Corinthians 5:21).* Please forgive me for being sinful. Please forgive me for making it necessary for Jesus to become sin for me, so that I might be redeemed and have a relationship and renewed fellowship with You. You have made a way for me to become righteous and for this I honor and thank You. In Jesus' name, I pray. Amen. 12.28.2013

Dear Father in Heaven,

As the year draws to an end and we look forward to a new start in the coming year, may we resolve to focus more on Christ. Please guide us with special opportunities to share The Word with someone that may not believe, has doubts or who is just simply uneducated and not familiar with the Bible. May each of us have boldness with the right words and right actions. Speak through those of us that know You; minister through us to someone who NEEDS to know You. Lord I ask that You grant each of us a part of YOUR touch in someone's life to the glory of Jesus and His name. Amen.

Dear Lord,

    Today I call upon Your name to trust You to provide for all Your children; to protect us from harm and evil, and to guide our steps each and every day. I praise You for all the things You have done for us. Your mercy endures forever and Your peace fills our souls. You are our Savior, our Sustainer, our Hope and our Comfort. I give thanks to You Lord. All glory and honor and praise to You this day of Thanksgiving and every day to come. With love and a grateful heart I pray to You and say thank You once more. Amen

Jesus wept. John 11:35

Dear Lord,

God I do not want to make You weep; I hope no one does. I pray that we are all aware of the things we do, say or think that make You sad.

PRIDE is an excessive belief in one's own abilities. May we set pride aside and give all glory to You for our talents and abilities.

ENVY is wanting what others have. May we all be happy with what You have provided us with and know that it is all we need.

GLUTTONY is the desire to consume more than we require. May everyone share their harvest and not hoard for themselves.

LUST is a craving for things such as sex, power and money. Lord, may Your children fight to even just think these sinful ways.

ANGER is the loss of rational self-control and desire to harm others. God I asked that we all think before we speak angry words or take physical action toward another human being. May anger subside with the calm of knowing that You are the Judge and You will handle the situation.

GREED is the desire for material wealth and gain. This is one of the main things that is destroying the world for it leads to pride, lust, and anger and lying tongues.

SLOTH is laziness and the avoidance of work.

I pray that **every** believer in Christ do good works for all of mankind and with desire in their hearts to please You. May the sins we have become blind to, be seen by us as through Your eyes. Lord, my prayer is that my brothers and sisters in Christ will avoid the deadly sins, follow Your Son with good works by spreading the Word and honoring our Father. May we never again make You sad. May we never make Jesus weep again. In the name of the Father, the Son and the Holy Spirit, I pray. Amen.

Dear God,

    Not everyone in this world has a chance to hide inside a home that provides heat from the winter chill and dryness from the rain or sleet and snow. As we lay under the covers of our warm comfy beds protected from the elements of Mother Nature, may we remember how blessed we truly are. May we not forget what You have asked of us, and take the time and make the effort to help others less fortunate by donating to the shelters or providing a warm meal to a family or lending a helping hand to a stranger on the street. An old coat that we no longer wear, a sweater we will never fit back into, a blanket that is folded on the shelf of a closet and not being used; items in the pantry; all things that could, and should, be given to someone in need. Lord, please give the lost souls that live on the streets the knowledge to realize there are many good people in the world with helping hands. I ask that You guide us to do our part for the needy. I ask that the needy do their part and have faith that You will provide for them if they only seek. Thank You, Lord for the shelter, food and warmth You have provided for me and my family and friends. Today may we share it all with someone else. In the name of Jesus, the Son of God. Amen.

Dear God,

    Sometimes I feel like I have poured myself into something or someone, and worked and fought for a cause, only to see no fruits for my labors. It may seem in vain, unappreciated and sometimes I receive accusations of trying to be in control or overbearing when in my heart I am just trying to help. I know that You can use my works to fulfill a greater purpose. Please don't let the labor of my heart and hands be in vain. Please let others understand that I am doing what You have asked of me for good purpose and eternal value. You, and only You, will receive the glory. Please bless the works of my heart and hands. Please empower me with wisdom and insight through Your Holy Spirit. Please guide me every step and every day, to have a part in reaching this world for You and ministering to those I love. In Jesus' name. Amen.

Dear Lord,

Thank You for the friends and family members that have defied their cancer, reclaimed their lives and are connecting with others to do the same. By Your divine touch they were miraculously healed. Please continue to give them strength to face the road ahead with treatments and possible fatigue or pain. Thank You for keeping Your arms wrapped around them and the friends and family members that, without interruption, stand beside these incredible people. You have walked with them, guided them and spoken to them in spirit by giving them strength, courage, hope and comfort in their time of need. Lord, there is not a place that Your hand cannot reach nor a heart You cannot touch. May we all be forever faithful and thankful for Your grace, Your love and Your promise. In the name of Jesus, thankfully I say Amen.

Fight like a girl – she did and she beat it.

Almighty Father,

Nothing brings me more happiness that being able to help someone in need. Whether it be spiritually, financially, physically or emotionally, it pleases me to see a person happy and doing well. It is a goal and an essential part of my life, but it can lead to some frustration as well as rewards. I am certain there are many that do the same as I try to do and sometimes feel this way.

Lord I pray those that are receiving help from another will appreciate the time, effort and gifts that have been given to them. May they understand that without the blessings You have given to US, WE would not be able to share what we have or what we may be able to do for them. I pray they learn to help themselves by making better choices, putting forth some effort to take care of pressing matters and not constantly relying on someone else or taking advantage of a person's generosity; and I hope and pray that they come to You in times of doubt or desperation.

Heavenly Father, I can only imagine how frustrated You must feel with the way Your children continually take advantage of all the grace, favor, and forgiveness You hand out to us on a daily basis. Even our earthly possessions are ours only because You have allowed them. I pray today that each of us takes the time to not only thank You for Your helping hand but that WE also start making better choices; that we start living a cleaner and more Christian life; that we allow less corruption to flow through our veins by not gossiping, judging or thinking bad thoughts; that we take care of Mother Earth as You so desire, and that we set Godly examples of love, faith and trust for our fellow brothers and sisters. You have been more than generous with us Lord. It is time for us to show our appreciation and love for You. It is time for those of us that have lost our way to come BACK to You with true faith in our hearts and know that You, with open arms, will always be here willing to help us. I ask that every day each of us reminds the other that FOR YOU, IN YOUR GLORY, we do our part as Christians to not only help others, but to also help ourselves. In the name of Your Son, Jesus, Amen.

Galatians 5:13-14 - You, my brothers, were called to be free. But do not use your freedom to indulge the sinful nature; rather, serve one another in love. The entire law is summed up in a single command: "Love your neighbor as yourself."

Dear God,

    Thank you for the changing seasons and the awesome wonder of nature that you have given us to enjoy and oversee. You have provided us with the cool fall breezes that are such a relief after a hot Texas summer. The leaves have turned from a beautiful green to the colors that fall brings; the flowers are the rusty warm shades of red, orange and gold and the harvest of pumpkins and crisp apples are ours for the taking. YOUR design, YOUR creation, all just for us. Thank You for this time of year when family and friends seem to draw closer and join us in the festive times full of abundant blessings we can share together. Thank You for meeting our needs. I pray for the less fortunate, that You will touch them and bring joy and provision into their lives. May each of us do as You command and help others; may we reach out to family, friend, or stranger and be one of their abundant blessings and glorify You. Thank You Lord for hearing me, for accepting my praise and for answering my heart's prayers. In Jesus' name. Amen.

Deuteronomy 6:4-9 – Hear, O Israel: The LORD our God, the LORD is one. Love the LORD your God with all your heart and with all your soul and with all your strength. These commandments that I give you today are to be upon your hearts. Impress them on your children. Talk about them when you sit at home and when you walk along the road, when you lie down and when you get up. Tie them as symbols on your hands and bind them on your foreheads. Write them on the doorframes of your houses and on your gates.

Dear God,

    I pray that accumulated inheritance never outweighs the personal legacy we have been left or that we leave behind for our children. May the footprints of our life leave not the talk of how much money we had, the house we lived in or the kind of car we drove. Instead may our children, like us, be left a legacy of lasting value that was added to the world around us.

    Today may we be a living legacy that provides a steady hand at the wheel of life so we may guide others through the storms as well as the gentle waters. When our name is spoken may we be thought of or remembered as a person of integrity, principles, good intentions and eternity in our hearts. Lord, I have come to appreciate the lessons You have taught me. My prayer for all of mankind is that they too will come to be in the place I am now; and that they will find in their heart, to live, as good stewards, to leave this world a better place than they found it. May we teach our children the meaning of integrity, to live by principles, to always have Good intentions, and to live with eternal life and love in their hearts. If they will live by these Godly values they too will leave a legacy behind for their children. Thank You for the Legacy that lives today. Amen.

Proverbs 22:1 "A good name is to be more desired than great wealth, Favor is better than silver and gold."

Dear Heavenly Father,

I pray today for the people whose lives have been turned upside down by an illness. Some are unable to work so they struggle financially. The cost of medicines has skyrocketed to the point that it makes it almost impossible to afford all of what is needed. Their transportation may need to be at someone else's convenience. Belongings are minimal; and most of what life has to offer is not affordable or, in some cases, not even enjoyable because of illness and sometimes just weakness. Lord, I come to You with a grateful heart because at the moment my health is such that I am able to help others that may not be as fortunate as myself. YOU have provided me with time to give to someone outside my home.

YOU have provided me with physical and emotional strength needed for such a task. I would not have that without You in my heart. YOU have provided me with finances that allows me to give monetarily. YOU paid it forward so we would be cleansed of our sins and have everlasting life. Now, today I pray that others as blessed as I am reach out to a family member, a friend, or our communities and follow in Your footsteps and "pay it forward". Our time may come sooner than expected; and we too may need someone as fortunate as WE are today to lend a helping hand. It is in Jesus' name I come to You today and say thank You for Your plan and thank You for that person in my life. I love You. Amen.

Everything we have is a gift from God. All good things are gifts from God. (1 Timothy 6:17)

Dear Lord,

  You have given each of us a talent; an important purpose that will benefit others, not just ourselves. May each of us serve You with the abilities You have given us so we may bring glory to Your name and blessings to others. That alone should prompt us to use our God-given gifts. Service to others will bring meaning and fulfillment to our lives in a way that wealth, power, possessions, and self-centeredness will never match. I pray that none of us limit our abilities to complete Your purpose; that we make good use of what has been given to us, no matter how great or small. May we all come to realize that the essence of Christian life is obeying and worshiping You and sharing our gifts. Thank you for my abilities Lord. May I use them wisely EVERYDAY, and may I be a blessing to others for Your glory. In the name of the Son of God, Jesus, Amen.

This is the day that You have made. I will rejoice and be glad in it. Psalm 118:24

Heavenly Father,

Today I choose to not focus on the negative surroundings of the news or gossip that I may hear. May I see the good and pure that come with all Your blessings. May my attitude encourage others, express faith, and glorify You. I thank You for the shining light of Your love that makes it possible for me to think positive. In Jesus' name, Amen.

Dear Lord,

Some criticize because I air my faith publicly by sharing verses from the Bible, written prayers and sometimes just an insight I might have. But I believe that I may be the only "Bible" someone ever reads. May the words I share always honor You. Thank You for pointing ME in the right direction. I asked for guidance to minister to others, instilling faith, and giving encouragement to them to walk alongside me, down the path, that leads them to You. I pray that I am always a living testament worth reading. In Christ Jesus, Amen.

Dear Lord,

    I want to live the life You planned for me. May the righteousness of Christ shine through me and be a light to this lost and dying world. Please show me how to use my gifts to influence others for You so they, too, may come to know You and experience Your joy, life-giving power, and forgiveness. Thank You for including me in Your plans and for loving me unconditionally. In Jesus name I pray, Amen.

Dear God,

    My eyes are open to see all that You have prepared for me, Lord. I love studying Your Word, and I love spending time in prayer with You in fellowship. Thank You for letting me know You. May I always be aware of all my special opportunities You give me to work for the Kingdom of God. As always, I ask for forgiveness for when I fail You. I ask that You give me the knowledge and strength to grow in faith daily. In the name of Jesus. Amen.

Good morning God,

Lord, please forgive us of backsliding into sin. We ask for new life in our hearts. Please restore our sensitivity to sin and help us to see sin as You see it. May we have strength and commitment to move forward with confidence and walk with You in obedience. Lord, we ask for forgiveness and for Your mercy and grace so that we may experience a true revival of a right spirit within ourselves. Thank You for favor and for hearing and receiving our prayers. With love in our hearts for our Savior, Amen.

He who conceals his sins does not prosper, but whoever confesses and renounces them finds mercy. (Prov 28:13)

Dear God,

    I pray that everyone that is reading this knows or learns to trust You even though they can't see the pathway in front of them. We must trust You to be all knowing, all loving and all powerful and to know that what You do for us and with us through You, will be done well. Paul wrote, *"Everything that does not come from faith is sin." (Romans 14:23).* Heavenly Father, please help us all to know that it is You that leads us through the darkness and that it is only in the darkness that we learn to walk with faith. In Jesus' name I pray. Amen.

Julo Spencer

Dear God,

    I feel so blessed today because you have let the rain come to my area of the world and watered the trees, grass and flowers; given drink to the birds and wild creatures that roam at night and You have filled our lakes. But Lord, there so many other areas that are suffering from drought where the earth is cracked and the lakes are low. Areas are burning from the dry ground and high winds. I pray that you will balance out the weather, so that a soft and steady rain would fall to water the dry earth; may the high winds become cool breezes that supply comfort from the heat. Lord please be with the men and women that fight the fires that are started by someone's carelessness and the elements that fuel the fires. Protect them, please. I pray for souls that like the ground are dry and desolate, that Your Spirit will tug at their heart strings and fill them with hope and joy and blessed assurance that You are with them always. I pray for Your children who are full of Your love and living in Your Word. I live in hope that they will share their life with others and continue to seek Your will and Your presence. Thank You, Lord for hearing my prayer. In Jesus' name. Amen.

Compliments of God

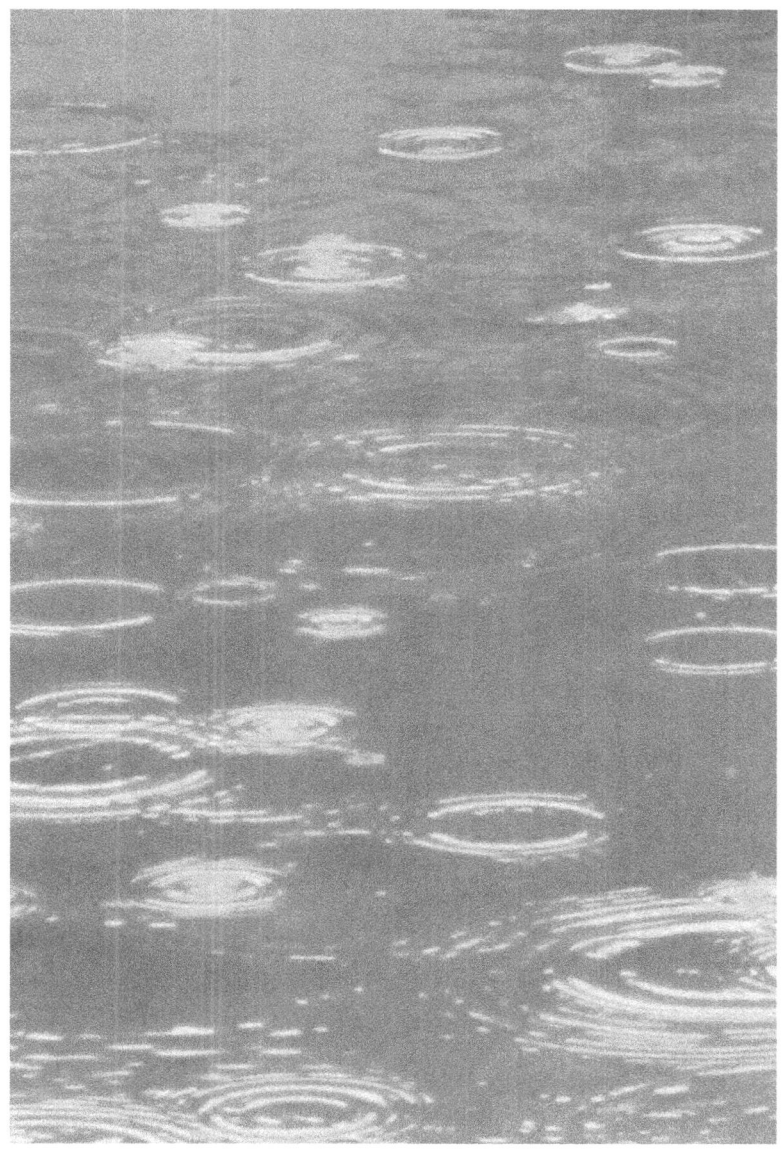

Good Friday morning Lord,

Today I look toward You and know that I truly depend on You to be my source of victory in life. You will and should receive all the glory. You bring so much richness to my life with Your love and grace. You make me a better person. May I always share You, Your love and Your Son's life with others. I ask that you protect my friends and family as they venture out over the weekend to be with their friends and families; on the road, in the sky and on the water. Thank You Lord and may we always remember that TGIF, is not for Friday, but to remind us that "today God is first"- In Jesus' name. Amen

Dear Lord,

I beg for Your forgiveness and ask that You send me out into the world to do Your will so that I may reach others for You. I want to accomplish what You want me to do. I pray for guidance always, Your wisdom and boldness so that I may influence others and carry out my Christian works. I pray for all who know You but are not close to You; that they grow closer by helping others in their families and communities. I also pray that we all see ourselves in need of our Savior and see the blessings You have bestowed upon us and know that You are God. It's these things I ask of You today, in Jesus' name, Amen.

Good morning God,

I pray this morning that everyone I know and everyone they know remembers that every day, You are in control of our lives. Control is OUR illusion. Truly we live in the delusion of having all control yet when the world comes crashing down on us, it is You we turn to. Your sovereignty is the attribute by which You rule the entire creation of mankind. You are all knowing AND all powerful. "God may Your will be done for the good of Your kingdom". Thank You for forgiving us when we act like the fools we are. May each of us find peace in knowing that You will provide. You will protect us. YOU are in control. In Jesus' precious name, Amen.

Dear God,

Thank you for sending special people into our lives. I can think of many who have meant so much to me and have been such an encouragement and inspiration. I appreciate them so much and miss the ones who have left this earth to be with You in eternity. Thank You, God, for the Holy Spirit, the Great Comforter who fills my heart, lifts my spirit, satisfies my soul, and brings your presence into my life. In Jesus' name I pray. Amen.

Dear Lord,

You have overcome the world; and because of Your promise, through You, we too can overcome it. I must rely on You when temptations enter my mind; when I feel discouraged or helpless; when I am angry or bitter, I must remember to "take it" to You through prayer and allow You to carry me through the storm once again. May we forever remain wise and follow these words. In the name of Jesus, I pray. Amen.

Dear Father in Heaven,

    Today may we pray for the lost in this world who do not communicate with You. They become so self-absorbed that they forget where to turn in the path of possible destruction. I pray right now for all of the families around the world who have grown apart, perhaps a couple on the verge of divorce or the child that rebels and decides to do it "their way". May each of them make time for one another; take time to listen and hear what might be going on in each other's lives and may they pray together about whatever the circumstances may be. God please reach down and tug on their hearts, speak to their minds, and show them the way. I pray that the root of their problems will be exposed and that through Your Word, rather than choosing the wrong direction to go, that they turn to You and follow the Light. May their hearts live as one, and I pray that these lost souls become healthy, happy, and God-honoring, communicating and loving families. Lord, please watch over and protect the families that are doing well by doing Your will. Thank You for Your love and guidance. In Jesus' name. Amen.

Dear Heavenly Father,

    This day brings heaviness to my heart and joy to my soul. Good Friday, the day that those of us who are followers of Christ, 'Christians', recognize the moment in history when Your Son, our Savior, was led to the Cross, to suffer crucifixion and physical death and experience separation from You because of our sin. I am so sorry that my sin and the sin of mankind made it necessary for such a sacrifice. I'm sorry that my sin caused Jesus such pain and grief and caused your heart to break. I thank You for providing a way for me to come to You through Jesus. I thank You that Good Friday was not the end, but that Jesus Christ resurrected on the third day and sits at your right hand today, interceding on my behalf and on behalf of all who come to Him with belief and faith and repentance. I remember today and I am grateful. For it is in the name of Jesus that I can lovingly come to You. Amen.

Dear God,

Ah, the sweet smell of fresh, cold water falling from the sky. Your gift of rain brings to mind Jesus' gift of love. Like the pouring rain, He pours out His love from Heaven. You give us nature's cleansing goodness and show evidence of His existence even when it is impossible to see Him. Thank you God for the rain. Amen.

Hello God,

Thank You for Your comforting promise that You will never leave nor forsake me. In times like today, I need that assurance. You are my Rock and my Salvation. I trust You, even when I feel like I cannot trust anyone else. I look up to You, because I know You will always be there for me, even if the whole world forsakes me. Thank You, so much, for Your love and dependability. You are awesome! With love and appreciation in my heart, I thank You. Amen.

Julo Spencer

Dear God,

"It's the simple things..." The simple things in life are the things that can irritate me and the things that can bring me the most pleasure. I want to thank You for the small things and the simple things. Please help me to stop and think before I react to little things that irritate me. Help me to always appreciate the simple things of life, for they are truly what I enjoy. Thank You for the beaches, mountains, lakes and forests; thank You for the light and warmth of the sun and the freshness and life in cooling rain; thank You for the wildflower so bright and pretty and the singing bird so beautiful; thank You for a child's love and a pet's devotion; thank You for a baby's breath and an old person's smile; thank You for a glass of cold water on a hot summer day. I could go on and on because there are endless things to be thankful for, but the greatest of all is love. Thank You for Your love. I love YOU. In Jesus' name. Amen.

Compliments of God

Dear God,

    Lord, as the day begins for some and ends for others may each of us look up and thank You for the abundance of "enoughness". I pray that no one begins their day with the notion they are deprived, a victim, with an attitude of entitlement or thoughts of "I deserve".   You have given us another day of sunshine, fresh air, creations that please our eyes, friends, family, a beating heart, a roof over our head, food, freedom and most precious to us, Your eternal love and guidance. "Thank You Lord, this is more than enough". Glory to God. Amen.

Heavenly Father,

You are the Master of life and death. You said I am the resurrection and the life and with the passing of a loved one, friend or family, we believe this with all our hearts. You have promised to be with the broken hearted in their time of sorrow. I ask that You please be with all of the family and friends, that so loved the one, that is now with You. We thank You that heaven is a real place and that when You said 'Today you will be with me in paradise', You were speaking to all of us who believe in You. Thank You for our final home; safe from pain, sickness and the sadness that touches so many. I pray that You help us because we are all Your children; help us so that our faith will not fail; help us so that we may always bring glory to You. Amen.

Nothing truly meaningful is achieved on the first attempt, and if that's where you stop, then failure is all you will have.

Dear Lord,

    I come to You today in prayer with the faith that You will get us through another day of failure. So many of us pray for a good outcome in a personal situation or something material that matters not in regards to being a success or a failure. God, please speak out to the ones that view failure as what "THEY" do not receive from You but rather what "YOU" do not receive from them. You give us life, yet we take it away; that is failure, and I am sorry. We commit adultery; that is failure, Lord, and I am sorry. We lie, cheat, and steal; that is failure, and I am sorry. We deny You in our public places; that is failure, and I am so sorry. You give us free will and we use it to destroy people, places and things; that is not success, that is failure and I am sorry. You are our Creator and Savior so I ask for forgiveness and guidance to this blameless society that we have created with our daily failures as Your children. I pray that You grant us the wisdom to know the difference in real success and failure. May we follow Your lead so that the world You created for us, will be what You want it to be. That will be our success and for that I thank You. In Jesus' loving name, Amen

Dear God,

Please forgive me of gossip that often spews from my lips. I desire a calm spirit that will allow me to not worry about the people and circumstances that surround me. I pray that I focus on Jesus, and, that I do not wrong anyone with my words or actions. Please replace any anger with peace so I may go about my day and accomplish Your will. May I be Your obedient child; a person who is a pleasure to be around and a loving witness, who speaks only words that sooth and uplift; pleasing to You and giving You all the glory. In Jesus' name I pray. Amen

Acts 17:24-The God who made the world and everything in it, being Lord of heaven and earth, does not live in temples made by man,

All God's Children

I have been fortunate enough to travel the world. The experiences of learning the different cultures, tasting the local cuisines and visiting many historical sites has been, well, just that, "an experience". I just returned from what I think might be my last trip overseas. As I stash away the pictures of my latest adventure into a folder on my computer, I begin to notice how many of these pictures look much like some I have taken at a different time in another part of the world. The mountains ranges and the melting snow from the mountain tops form the beautiful falls that feed the lakes; the sight and sound of the fast-moving waters that rush over the river rocks; the foliage on the trees and vines that change colors with the seasons; the supply of rainfall that builds lush green fields and supplies the animals with food. All the same kind of different. It's as if during the time of Creation, God "copied and pasted" a little bit of Spain into Colorado... or maybe the other way around.

The foods of the various cultures may be prepared differently, but they are the same ingredients in the east as they are in the western part of the world. Again the same kind of different.

Artifacts from the Holy Land, pieces of armor, an arrowhead or maybe a uniform worn by a soldier that fought in a battle during the time of Troy, the Civil War or more recently in Afghanistan, are all on display in the museums around the world. Old buildings where someone famous lived or worked; churches and Cathedrals that date back to 11th and 12th centuries. Walls, ruins, statues…..all representative of the time in which they were constructed; plaques baring the history behind the fallen structure or the man or woman that became part of the story and will live on in our hearts and minds for years to come. Yes, once again the same kind of different in each part of this world.

I have been the typical tourist just about everywhere I have been. I try to pack the cutest of clothes to wear even though I am surrounded by people that I will never see again…doubt that they care what I have on. I equip myself with all the chargers for every device possible to stay in touch with the other side of the world; there's the ever famous fanny pack that, laugh if you must, does come in handy when toting all the necessary credentials needed to prove, I am who I say I am. I have a camera hanging off of one shoulder and a bag of another sort, to carry whatever else I THINK I need, off of the other shoulder. I search for "that" special item, typical of the artisans of the area I am visiting, to add to the décor of my home. Our house is dotted with various pieces of artwork or glassware from the many countries and regions I have toured. I hunt for the perfect souvenir for someone back home. I have every "I "heart" (wherever)" coffee mug available, and of course I always buy the "all I got was a T-shirt" shirt for Duncan and Gunnar.

However, let me put all the silly tourist stuff aside for a moment. Allow me, if you will, to tell you, what my most loved attraction in the world is. It's the people. The one's I see and watch for a moment in a public place. The one's that service the visitors; or the kind strangers on the street that give directions or information when asked. The people that share the stories about their city, their culture and sometimes their family. It is the long-time resident that makes my trips interesting by openly sharing things not found in any tourist brochure. I have discovered there is common ground between nations; the most common being the belief that God does exist. What I see and now realize is that the world is full of Believers. Millions upon millions that proudly claim their faith; God loving and God fearing people who pray just like I do. Millions who believe that Jesus died for our sins, that God forgives, God heals and that Heaven is real. They read the Bible and believe the words that are written in it. They do not doubt the Promise that has been made to us. They do not doubt that God WILL send His son for us again.

Faithfully, I thank You Lord for allowing me to see and meet so many of the beautiful people that occupy this world. I not only say, God bless America, I say, God bless all the Believers the world over.

Dear God,

Lord, who created mankind in Your image, You sure made a colorful world of people! As I stop and watch and reflect on the people I see, I notice how everyone is unique. Sometimes I'm frustrated by others' personalities and actions; other times I am blessed; still other times I am amused. The fact is, though we were made in Your image, You gave us each a will of our own and instilled different gifts, personalities, and potential within us. How boring it would be if we were all just alike. The "spice" of life is made up of all those different people, with different ideas and various contributions. Thank You for caring enough that we are not Your puppets, but are unique individuals; each called to fill special places in Your great plan for our lives. I pray that You will keep my eyes open, my mind alert and my will in tune so that I will use all You have given me. May I use Your gifts, personality, skills, and desires, to the best of my ability to reach the lost and glorify You. Please forgive my past failures and empower me today for all You want to do through me. In Jesus' name. Amen.

Dear Heavenly Father,

I pray that all of us slow down and smell the roses so we may enjoy what You have created and put before us. May we free our hearts from hatred, free our minds from worries, live simply, expect less; and, most of all have a deep relationship with You. In Your precious name I pray this simple prayer that will make a world of difference in our lives. Amen.

There probably is no better way to start a day than by saying "thank You, Lord".

Our Dear Lord,

    I thank You God for giving me another day, another chance to become a better individual, and another chance to give and experience love. Thank You for another unused opportunity to do it right. Of all the promises in the Bible, the ones that often mean the most to us are the promises that offer hope at the end of affliction; a light at the end of the tunnel. Those promises that tell us "It's worth it; walk with Me; trust Me and wait with Me, I will reward you." No need to ask for favors for I know everything comes when the time is perfect. Thank You God for listening, for Your patience with us and for always being next to us. In Christ name I pray. Amen.

Dear Father,

    My prayers go out to all the families today that get sidetracked by their own desires. The almighty dollar pushes them towards the quest for more, and what others may think of them, while trying to 'climb the ladder' of success. They overload themselves with activities, and if it's not satisfying enough, they add even more activities to their already-busy schedule. They work too hard. Some suffer from illness. Others take on challenges and sometimes encounter problems beyond their imagination. There are so many distractions these days that take us away from what You want for us. Lord, I pray that everyone acknowledges their lack of time with You and makes a commitment to put You before their own desires. May their first thoughts of each new day be of You. May they spend time in prayer; reading and studying Your word as they look forward to a more positive outlook of the hours ahead of them. I pray they acknowledge You as the only true answer to less stress. If they are reading this devotional right now, they have time. In the name of Jesus. Amen.

Dear God,

I have felt emotional pain and I have experienced physical pain. I have seen how pain can change a person's life. I hope and pray that I will always be able to reach out to others; to think of them and not myself; to think of You rather than focus on my own pain. When I am able to reach out and help someone else my spirit is filled with joy, happiness, and satisfaction. It takes my mind off my own pain and problems, and directs it to a better perspective. Please use me to ease the pain of all others. In Jesus' name I pray. Amen.

Dear Lord,

Another day has come and gone. As I watch the sun set over this beautiful land of ours, I see that it too is tired. It slowly drops from the sky as if it is closing tired eyes giving us the night to rest.

The bright light of the moon will take over as the stars dance about. Hours will pass and the moon and stars will bow out and, once again, allow the sun to rise and start yet another glorious day of Your miraculous plan. The only words that come to mind are "thank You". In the name of the Son, Jesus. Amen

"Everyone who calls on the name of the Lord will be saved" (Acts 2:21).

Dear Lord,

    Please forgive me of my sins. My lack of good judgment has made me sin many times in my lifetime, yet You always forgive me and put me back on track by offering me love, grace, and through the sacrifice of Your Son, Jesus, You have washed away my sins and given me the promise of eternal life. I want to be right with YOU and to always make You proud of me as a child of God. So this morning, Lord, I ask that you please forgive me AGAIN. Please know that I love You; and that, in my heart, my faith lies in You and You alone. Please give me the desire to spread the Word and to conduct myself always in a Godly manner. Please give me knowledge of daily words so I may talk the talk, and may I follow the footprints in the sand, and forever walk the walk. In the name of the Father, the Son and the Holy Ghost, Amen.

Dear God,

    You have given your children the ability to have "free will". Sometimes we do not choose to use it with respect for You, thus leading us to make mistakes in life. We do not think things through with clarity and purpose; never considering who it might hurt or effect; and certainly without realizing the consequences we must pay. We make mistakes because, we are, after all, human. God, I pray, that we all "own up" to our mistakes in life and that the results of our bad judgment leads us to a life of dedication and willingness to serve You. May we look to You for the answers to make things right, so we will move forward and live a life that is more pleasing to You; one full of love and guidance by Your hand. Thank You, Lord, for Your mercy and grace. In the name of Jesus. Amen.

Dear God,

That big orange ball was beautiful this morning as it rose and lit up the heavenly blue sky that You have created for us. Glory to You for all things created by Your hand and thank You for another day of waking up and experiencing the sunshine. In Jesus' name, Amen.

Photo by Ana DeLeon Sikes

Julo Spencer

God helps those who help themselves...

Dear God,

    You have given us a connection of love between our souls and You. When we approach You with legitimate desires and speak from our hearts as a child of God, and not a beggar, our prayers are answered. We make requests, express thankfulness, offer praise, intercede on behalf of others, and offer petition. You will act if we are willing to do our part.

    Lord my prayer today is that, as Your children, we all pray in a way that pleases You. Guide us so that our prayers are answered by doing our part as Christians. We must work for our daily bread with Godly effort so at the end of the day we can say "a job well done" and wreak the rewards. Our good health requires us to take care of our bodies and we should not knowingly damage our health for personal pleasures. You give us opportunities to learn and gain wisdom, but we must help ourselves through the natural process of study. And we MUST use our knowledge to spread the gospel and teach the lost. We know because we come to You in prayer that You bless our work and it accomplishes GOOD that may not have been accomplished had we not prayed.

    Every day may we do OUR part and sincerely serve You, our Lord and Savior, so we will truly come to know You and fully understand the power of prayer. In the name of our Heavenly Father, Jesus. Amen.

Heavenly Father,

Please forgive me for basing my self-worth on what I own, how large my bank account is, where I have been or even how many friends I might have. I ask that You guide me so I will know and show my self-worth because I was made in YOUR image and that alone makes me more valuable than ANYTHING on this earth. I pray that everyone knows that they are no more valuable to You now than the day they were born. Our greatest riches cannot and will never compare with knowing You and your Son *"I consider everything a loss compared to the surpassing greatness of knowing Christ Jesus my Lord" (Philippians 3:7-8).* Please forgive us for being influenced by the media that sends messages designed to create dissatisfaction and lust for what we don't have. May we ALWAYS know that our purpose for our existence is to know You. In Jesus' name I pray, Amen.

Dear Lord,

So many of Your children are suffering from vanity these days, and most of us are guilty of muttering a vanity prayer. In our hearts we know that pampering ourselves and entitlement beliefs are products of vanity and have very little value. We believe happiness comes from looking younger or being high-school-skinny again. The years have caused some of us not to hear or see well yet we are too vain to allow or provide assistance with our natural senses. Memories have become vague causing frustration and for some, confusion.

Lord let us not forget that aging is a natural process and something You have tried to prepare us for in life. Please forgive us for displaying such self-importance. To help others and not boast or show pride for one's successes or generosity is the inside beauty YOU want to see and for us to see in ourselves. Please help us know that how we may see each other on the outside is not the way of Jesus' teachings. Give us the insight to include a daily spiritual examination and a search for what is eternal.

Please let us realize what things are fleeting and not invest or waste our time on things that do not last. Rather than pray for ourselves; to be vain by trying to seek the youth that we once had or to be boastful and full of pride, let us seek Your word and follow the guidance the Bible gives us to help others. May none of us ever let our outward appearance become more important than the search for internal realities.

Lord, may the true beauty of life come from Your love and the love we show for others. May we know that Your promise alone is enough for all of us to age gracefully. In the name of Jesus. Amen.

Lord,

I come to You in the Name of Jesus asking that You will bring peace and comfort to anyone that has received devastating news. May You grant peace and understanding to all of life's situations. Thank You for Your wonderful promises. With them we are able to face the world and overcome challenges and temptation. I pray that all of Your children live each day with purpose and passion and their belief in You will help them meet their expectations.

Please remind each of us to take it to our Lord in prayer and allow You to carry us through the hours of each day until the days turn into weeks, weeks into months, and months into years. As we experience the unexplained miracles in our life, in other's lives, I hope and pray that we see this as Your Work and that we share these Miracles with others so that we may model ministry as Jesus modeled it. And with this Lord, I pray that You please make me a vessel of YOUR power, not simply a vessel of words. In the name of the Son of God, Jesus, I thank You. Amen.

Dear Lord,

Thank You for being the all-knowing, all powerful Ruler of the Universe and for looking out for us with Your perfect love. Thank You for being so trustworthy and for having our best interest at heart. Lord may we always surrender our will to You; in good times and in bad. Though it is difficult to give up our independence when things are not going as WE have planned, we must submit to Your will and know who is in control. Please help all of us with that concept in prayer and not wait until we hit rock bottom to talk to You. May we pray for others to come to You so they, too, will understand Your will and gain knowledge through scripture and learn that You will lead them in the right direction. May everyone believe You, our Lord, never abandons those that trust in You. Life is all about Your will, and the sooner we all learn that the sooner our prayers will touch Your heart to whom nothing is impossible. As always, thank You for listening, for answering and for always loving us. In the name of Jesus. Amen.

The World Has Changed; Not the Word

I was challenged a couple of days ago with an issue that I won't go into, but the words of the Bible were part of a heated discussion I was in. The person I was, for lack of a better word, arguing with said to me that the Bible was written over 2000 years ago and the words do not apply to us today. I agree the Book was written 2000 years ago, but the words have never changed no matter how many times they have been translated or published. I was appalled and amazed that this person thought they have new meaning. I am a Christian but I am a sinner too just like everyone is. I backslide just like my neighbor does, and there are times when I don't act in the manner that God would like for me. But it is the words of the Bible that get me back on track; the same words that were written 2000 years ago.

Dear God,

The Bible, or as I like to call it, The Good Book, was written over 2000 years ago and many consider it outdated or old fashion. Lord, I pray for everyone reading this prayer today to open the Bible and read Your spoken words that were inscribed so many years ago and realize that the scriptures and lessons are the same in today's world as they were in centuries past. Only man has changed; and, with that, so has the world. Thank You, Lord, for the forgiveness of our ignorance. Life is not easier than it was 2000 years ago. In fact, it is harder than ever. May we view the Bible as a book of protection and well-meaning advice. Give us the desire to read, understand, and follow the messages. The Bible is not irrelevant. It stands the test of time. There is no issue You do not address if we look hard enough. May we read with wanting eyes and understand that the answers needed IN TODAY'S WORLD, like the blood You shed for us, are written in Red. In Jesus' name, Amen.

Julo Spencer

Dear God,

    It seems that I find it better, more personal, to pray with no man made roof over my head. I stand on the edge of the Canyon with only blue sky above and take a deep breath of the fresh air. I look around me with wonderment, and with arms wide open I say thank You for ALL of this! No building full of people, no plate being passed, and the only hymns being sung are the natural sounds of Your Creation. This is the church of God. It is the perfect quiet time for a walk down a path with You. I will clear my head of any clutter, worries, or gossip. Today I choose to have a conversation of thankfulness, peace, praise and gratitude for all You have given, for the beauty before me and for the friends that are here sharing this with me. Lord, I do pray that others find a quiet place in nature; a path to walk down with You today. May they take time to look up to the heavens even if it is a cloudy day because beyond those clouds is the same blue sky that I am seeing. May they embrace all of Creation and praise You. May they reflect on life and all it holds for them, and with love in their hearts may they give thanks. In the name of Your perfect Creation, Your Son Jesus. Amen.

Compliments of God

Dear God,

    Thank You for answered prayers. For the child that was on the wrong path but is now seeking You; for the friend or family member that is ill but is now on the road to recovery; for a furry friend that was lost and returned home safely; for a much needed job; for travelers on the road that met their destination without harm. For a saved marriage. All because we asked, You answered. THANK YOU. In Jesus' name, Amen.

Compliments of God

In today's world of high-speed technology, we connect with each other, we play games with a friend, and we can quickly obtain information on any subject with the click of a button. Yet often, we are looking for more than information. We're seeking guidance to know which decision will lead us to our highest good. Thankfully, we have access to divine wisdom which is far more reliable than an Internet search engine. Within each of us lies a great storehouse of knowledge. It is the wisdom of the Universe. May we recognize it is the wisdom of God.

Compliments of God

LIFE IS SHORT AND TIME IS SWIFT

As the golden years rapidly sneak up on me, I feel myself becoming more sentimental, giving a softer touch and definitely more aware of the ways of the world and all it offers. I find my patience more at ease with those little things that once bothered me. I can look back on my childhood with clarity and smile with what I have gained from the way I was raised. Even the bitterness I once felt toward someone has subsided, and I look for more pleasant memories that will make me smile at the thought of them. Love has taken on new meaning from when I was young; the passing giddy infatuation I had in my youth has turned to names etched on my heart forever.

When I pray, I mean what I say. My conversations with God are as if He really is my "best friend forever". There was a time in my life when I was afraid of the unknown. Now I go full speed ahead and challenge it head on. Death might be the biggest fear anyone ever faces; but, as we all know, it is inevitable. Right now I know God is preparing me for my time with Him. The body has slowed down; my mind tends to forget, and the old eyes and ears have begun to fail me. These are all God's plan for preparing me for the twilight years and my end to life as I know it. I will admit I am not ready to leave this earth. There are things to do, people to see, and places to go. But when my time comes, I pray that God takes a look at me and says,

"You were lost but, by choice, you took the path I prepared for you and found your way. I won you over because you learned to let Me take care of you. You asked my forgiveness and you kept your faith; you spread my Word, and you learned to believe in the Promise I made so many centuries ago. And I do believe you even wrote your story with Me in your heart, hoping and praying that you could bring ONE more of my children to Me. Yes, I think you're okay in My book".

I have never felt the sweetness of the Lord more than I do today. I reflect on my past, but I look forward to my future. I don't think God is finished with me just yet!

For I am convinced that neither death nor life, neither angels nor demons, neither the present nor the future, nor any powers, neither height nor depth, nor anything else in all creation, will be able to separate us from the love of God that is in Christ Jesus our Lord. -- Romans 8:38,39 (NIV)

My story may not be unique to the person reading it, but it is unique to me, just as your story is to you. We all have a past; some more pleasant than others, but if you learn to truly walk with God by your side, trusting His ever-loving guidance, you too will walk with lifted spirits, understanding, forgiveness, peace and you will soon discover you are not alone. I pray that you are as blessed as I am, and learn the greatest of all; to love.

www.ingramcontent.com/pod-product-compliance
Lightning Source LLC
LaVergne TN
LVHW051727080426
835511LV00018B/2931